CHARLES RAVINSKI

SKATE

OBSE
SSION

Flammarion

Contents

From Hobby

When it first emerged, no one could have predicted that skateboarding would become a global success. What began as a simple pastime has evolved into a discipline practiced around the world by all kinds of riders, with a huge market behind it. So how did skateboarding become the phenomenon that it is today?

It began with a counter-culture movement: when the waves weren't cooperating, young Californian surfers came up with the idea of hitting the sidewalk on wooden planks fitted with wheels.

Guess What ? Before it was given its current name (literally meaning "skating on a board"), skateboarding was referred to as "sidewalk surfing," due to its roots in the waves of California.

This movement grew into a genuine subculture—
or even multiple subcultures: riders came
together based on shared interests and
established an edgy new style that captivated
a wider public from the outset. While some
riders invented increasingly complex tricks,
others created their own brands. In doing so,
they wrote the first chapters of skateboarding's
remarkable history.

In our era of mass pop culture, skateboarding
can now be found in a multiplicity of spheres—
from fashion to film, from music to art, or from
video games to the Olympic games—to the point
of becoming a worldwide . . . obsession.

to
Sub-
culture

The
Essen

Like any self-respecting sport, skateboarding has its own particular equipment and terminology. You can't talk about or understand this universe without knowing the basics. So, let's get started by going over the key terms, tricks, and gear.

ntials

Anatom

Nose
The front of
the skateboard.

Deck
The area of the skateboard that the rider
stands on. The deck is usually made of seven
layers of bonded maple wood. It may look
symmetrical, but this is just an illusion:
the nose and tail are angled differently
to make certain tricks easier to perform.

Wheels
A skateboard's
polyurethane
wheels are mounted
on ball bearings.
Form, diameter, and
hardness vary
depending on the
terrain and a rider's
specific practice.

Tail
The back of the
skateboard.

y of a Skateboard

Trucks
These metal parts hold the axle and wheels to the deck. They let the rider swivel and perform a type of trick known as a "grind."

Griptape
This abrasive, self-adhesive material, similar to sandpaper, keeps riders' feet securely on the board so they can maintain control while performing tricks.

Hardware
The nuts and bolts used to connect the trucks to the deck.

Guess What ? Skaters get pretty obsessed with their gear. Some attach their wheels back to front to hide the brand logo, while others choose a different colored bolt or cut a design in their griptape to differentiate the front of the deck from the back.

Skatebo
Term

Trick, slam, bail, sketchy, goofy— skateboarding has a vocabulary all its own. Here are the essential expressions you should know to avoid coming across as a "poser."

Bail

Act of interrupting a move that feels like it's about to go wrong. Although frustrating, bailing is preferable to slamming.

Drop in

To go from a flat platform into a steep transition, such as a bowl or half-pipe.

Fakie

When a skater rides backwards, but in their normal stance (regular- or goofy-footed).

Goofy

A skater is said to be goofy-footed if they normally stand on the deck with their right foot forward.

Land

To complete a trick with both feet on the deck. When a rider lands perfectly, with a foot over each truck, this is known as **landing bolts**— the ultimate goal.

Mob

Used to describe tricks performed with bad style.

Obstacle

Any feature at a skatepark that can be used by skaters to do tricks. This could include rails, ledges, ramps, half-pipes, among others.

Part

Short video, or an excerpt from a video, showing a rider's impressive tricks set to a soundtrack.

Poser

Someone who dresses like a skater, without practicing skateboarding regularly or knowing the codes.

barding
inology

Regular
A skater is said to be regular-footed if they normally stand on the deck with their left foot forward.

Riding
Slang term for skateboarding. Skateboarders are known as **riders.**

Sesh
Short for a skateboarding session.

Sketchy
Used to describe an imperfect or poorly executed trick.

Slam
To fall while rolling or attempting a trick.

Snake
To cut off other riders waiting to skate an obstacle at a spot.

Spot
Urban location suitable for skating (authorized or not), where riders gather.

Switch
When a skater rides with the opposite foot forward and performs tricks with the opposite foot to normal. Switch tricks are more difficult than those performed in the normal stance.

Team
Group of skaters sponsored by a brand.

Trick
Skateboard maneuver.

Try
Attempt to perform a trick. **"First try!"** is the cheer heard when someone completes a trick on the first go.

Basic

Riding is great, but performing tricks is even better. Tricks lie at the very heart of the sport and provide constant fuel for battles. Mastering these moves demands perseverance, which makes each new trick that a skater learns a hard-won victory.

Ollie

The mother of all tricks, this move consists of jumping while maintaining contact between the board and the feet. To successfully perform this seemingly magical trick, the skater pushes down on the deck's tail until it hits the ground (the **pop**), while dragging their front foot up the board along the griptape.

Tricks

Flip

The skateboard is spun 360º on its lengthwise axis. There are two types of flip: the **kickflip** (initiated with the front foot) and the **heelflip** (initiated with the heel).

Manual

The skater rolls while balanced on the skateboard's back wheels. The variation performed on the front wheels is called a **nose manual**.

Grab

The skater holds the skateboard with their hand or hands while in the air. **Nosegrab, tailgrab, melon grab** (using the front hand to grab the heel side of the board), etc. refer to the part of the board that the skater grabs and the hand used.

Shove-it

(or **shuvit**, also known as a **backside shove-it/shuvit**)

The skateboard is turned 180º on its vertical axis, using the back foot, which pushes backwards to spin the board around behind the skater. The **pop shove-it** begins like an ollie: the deck's tail is pushed down against the ground and the board spun 180º. During a **frontside shove-it**, the board rotates in the opposite direction: the skater pushes forwards with their back foot to spin the board around in front of them.

Grind
A move that involves sliding one or both trucks along an object.

Wallride
The skater uses momentum
to ride vertically along a wall.

Endless combinations
Once a skater has learned the basic tricks, the sky's the limit.
Slides, grinds, and manuals can be performed before or after
a flip or a shove-it; a grab can be done during a rotation.
The goal is to create increasingly complex sequences.

Riders can also play around with foot placement
and direction of movement by inverting their stance
(the **switch**), popping the nose of the skateboard instead
of the tail (the **nollie**), or riding backwards (the **fakie**).

Slide
A move that involves sliding the underside of the deck along a rail, wall, or other obstacle.

The
Radica
of
Skatebo

al Rise
oarding

From its makeshift beginnings to its inventive adolescence and eventual professionalization, skateboarding has had an unstoppable rise in popularity over the years. As a sport, a style, and a culture, it has stood the test of time, sparking revolutions at every step. Here are the key moments that have shaped this unique phenomenon.

The
1950s:
Sidewalk

The first skateboards were simple homemade objects, invented by surfers to use on dry land when the waves were flat. It took about a decade for the skateboard to evolve beyond its humble beginnings.

Although the skateboard's precise origins remain uncertain, a common thread runs through every version of its history: when the waves weren't cooperating on the beaches of California, surfers came up with the idea of attaching wheels to a plank of wood so they could ride the asphalt. This was in the early 1950s, and the first "sidewalk surfers" began to appear on the streets.

Gear was basic at the time. Boards were made from shortened surfboards or pieces of wood retrieved from shipping crates. Wheels were metal and were attached to the board with whatever was on hand, including leather straps, nails, and hardware salvaged from roller skates.

With equipment like this, complex tricks were out of the question. Early skaters stuck to weaving and sliding their way down the sidewalk. But the thrill of the ride, already enticing, was clearly felt. More importantly, these early days of skateboarding embodied the sport's fundamental values of freedom, creativity, and the desire to defy limits.

Guess What ?

The very first skaters took to their boards . . . barefoot. A carryover from surfing, this practice gave riders more control because they could grip the edge of the deck with their toes.

Surfers

Like all good inventions, the skateboard eventually caught the attention of entrepreneurs. In 1957, a Californian retiree named Alf Jensen began salvaging wooden oven paddles used by a local bakery and attaching metal wheels to them. He marketed these rudimentary skateboards, with a humorous nod to their origins, as Bun Boards. Two years later, the Roller Derby Skate Company followed his lead and began marketing the first industrially produced skateboard throughout the US. These two burgeoning companies stoked enthusiasm for skateboards, which greatly contributed to their widespread popularity.

In 1962, Bill Richards, owner of the Val Surf Hollywood store, convinced the Chicago Roller Skate Company to send him spare roller skate parts, which he attached to boards that he then sold in his shop. The same year, the Patterson Forbes company released its own skateboard model with improved trucks. These technological advances turned

The 1960s: Scali

In the 1960s, the skateboard moved away from its homemade roots. Thanks to the first mass-produced boards and specialized magazines, "sidewalk surfing" spread inland from the coast to conquer the city.

the skateboard into more than just a means of transport and paved the way for slaloming and freestyling.

In 1963, Larry Stevenson was working as a lifeguard on a California beach when he observed a group of teenagers skating in a parking lot. He was convinced that this unconventional object had serious sales potential and created his own brand, Makaha Skateboards. To outpace his competitors,

ng Up

he threw everything into marketing: at the time, he was already publishing *Surf Guide Magazine*, which he used to run ads for Makaha, and he sponsored the first skate contest at Hermosa Beach, assembling the first-ever skateboard team. In doing so, he almost single-handedly laid the foundations for the skateboarding market. A year later, the surf legend Hobie Alter created Hobie Skateboards and put together his own team: the Hobie Super Surfer skateboard team.

Facing page   **Skateboard** brought to the UK from the US by British music producer Andy Wickham, 1963.

Above   Young skaters on the streets of Chicago, 1965.

On the heels of mass production came media coverage. The first skateboarding magazine, *The Quarterly Skateboarder*, appeared in 1964. The following year, in a now iconic article, *Life* magazine wrote about the emergence of skateboarding in the streets of New York and introduced the skateboard to the general public. Also in 1965, the first skateboarding film was released: *Skaterdater*, directed by UCLA student Noel Black, recounts the story of two riders who engage in a skating duel following a romantic dispute.

Several months later, one of the most influential brands in the history of skateboarding was created. Paul Van Doren, along with his brother Jim and two investors, created the Van Doren Rubber Company, whose name would later be shortened to Vans. Although the brand eventually became an icon, it got off to a humble start and skaters wouldn't adopt it for another decade.

Vans's underwhelming debut was symbolic of the difficult period to come: in the late 1960s, skateboarding's popularity plummeted, likely caused by the heavy and impractical equipment, its reputation as a dangerous activity, and the basic ways of riding (slalom and freestyle) that soon got boring.

After a spectacular start, skateboarding was on the verge of dying out. Luckily, it was saved by two key inventions and a group of riders who would change everything.

Above   Poster for the film *Skaterdater*, 1965.

Facing page   Patti McGee on the cover of *Life* magazine, May 1965, which featured an article that began as follows: "That thing 19-year-old Pat McGee is balancing on is a skateboard, the most exhilarating and dangerous joy-riding device this side of the hot rod."

Skateboarding's first introduction to a mainstream audience was hardly a favorable one. In 1965, *Life* magazine described the skateboard as "a teeter-totter on wheels" and skateboarding as "the new fad and menace" that "gives the effect of having stepped on a banana peel while dashing down the back stairs." Not exactly a glowing endorsement!

Below   Skateboard by the Roller Derby brand, produced in Illinois, c. 1960.

LIFE

The craze and
the menace of
SKATEBOARDS

San Diego's Pat McGee,
national girls' champion,
does a handstand on wheels

MAY 14 · 1965 · 35¢

The 1970s: A Cool Comeback

After a nearly fatal decline in popularity, skateboarding radically transformed over the next decade. Gone were the innocence of the early days and the elegant glide of sidewalk surfing. In the 1970s, skateboarding became more extreme and conquered new ground.

Once again, it all began in California—in Dogtown, to be precise, a stretch of west Los Angeles that runs between Venice Beach and Santa Monica. Back then, Dogtown was a far cry from the sun-drenched picture-postcard setting it is today: the area's abandoned ports and beaches frightened away tourists and were only frequented by a few hardcore surfers. It was in this neighborhood, in 1973, that a surf shop named Zephyr opened. Its team, the Z-Boys, would go on to become a legend.

So, who were the famous Z-Boys? They were local, working-class kid surfers who didn't always have the means to travel and chase the best waves. Forced to adapt, they practiced a more aggressive and unpredictable style of surfing. When they started skating, they brought this same style—defined by tight turns, high speed, and bold moves—to the streets. The pioneers of sidewalk surfing were skeptical, but the younger generations and competition juries

Facing page   Tony Alva,
member of the Z-Boys,
skating an empty swimming
pool—the ancestor of
the half-pipe.

Above   Jay Adams,
member of the Z-Boys.

Right   Skater performing
a 5-0 in an improvised
skatepark in London, 1978.

loved it: at a national contest held in Del Mar in 1975, half of the finalists were members of the Z-Boys.

These athletic feats were paired with a style transformation: jeans, Vans shoes, and colorful T-shirts were de rigueur. The younger generation was enthralled by the Z-Boys' style. The Dogtown cross, a visual created by artist C. R. Stecyk III, could be found graffitied on the walls of Venice and emblazoned on the undersides of skateboard decks. What began as a local epiphenomenon took on national, then international proportions. Skateboarding spread to Tahiti, Australia, and Europe.

The stardom of the Zephyr crew was changing skateboarding for good. And the revolution was about to benefit from some unexpected weather conditions.

It was 1976, and California was experiencing record-breaking drought. Many backyard swimming pools had been emptied to conserve water. The Z-Boys converged on these makeshift ramps, and other riders in the area quickly followed suit, leading to

Left   Skater performing a handstand in the street in London, 1976.

Above   Deck printed with the Dogtown skaters' iconic cross symbol.

Facing page, top   Skaters in an abandoned swimming pool in Cambridge, Massachusetts, 1978.

Facing page, bottom   Urethane wheel by French brand Banzaï.

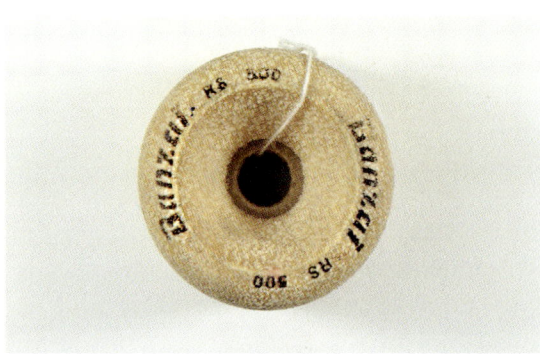

handling and expanded the repertoire of possible tricks. Wheels got an overhaul, too: the Cadillac Wheels brand, founded by Frank Nasworthy, released the first polyurethane skateboard wheels, which were more comfortable and versatile than their metal predecessors. And there were more places to skate, as skateparks started popping up all over the US.

As the decade drew to a close, skateboarding reached new heights. Now considered the very essence of cool, the sport was ready to take on pop culture.

the invention of vert skateboarding (literally "vertical skateboarding"). The same year, across the country in Florida, a young man named Alan Gelfand, known as "Ollie," managed to jump over the edge of a skatepark ramp, his feet still on his deck, without placing a hand on his board. In his honor, Gelfand's friends named the revolutionary trick after him—and so the "ollie" was born, and with it the practice of skateboarding as we know it today.

As skaters became more acrobatic, skateboarding gear improved. Boards now had a kicktail: a raised back that improved

Guess What?

The Dogtown skaters owe their fame in part to images captured by their official photographer—who was fourteen years old at the time. Glen E. Friedman attended the same middle school as several members of the Z-Boys and began photographing their performances after class. Encouraged by his friends, he decided to send his photos to *SkateBoarder Magazine*, which selected one to illustrate a subscription ad.

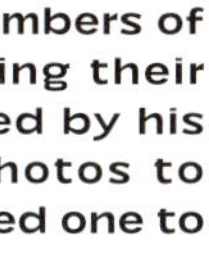

Left   Per Welinder, member of the Powell Peralta team, at the Del Mar Skate Ranch, California, 1984.

Facing page   A teenage Tony Hawk at the Del Mar Skate Ranch, California, 1982.

All good things must come to an end: as the 1970s drew to a close, the Z-Boys disbanded, and the most influential among them created their own empires. One such skateboarder-turned-entrepreneur was Tony Alva, who called his new brand Alva Skates. Another was Stacy Peralta, who teamed up with George Powell, a skateboarder who held an engineering degree, to create one of the most prominent companies in the history of skateboarding: Powell Peralta.

Many factors contributed to the pair's success. The first was their brand logo: a skeleton with red eyes peering out of a pair of yellow wings, which was perfectly in tune with the tastes of a generation about to spend the decade headbanging to Metallica. The duo's second advantage was the Powell Peralta team, nicknamed the Bones Brigade, in reference to the bone-colored wheels manufactured by the brand. It included riders who would eventually become the first skateboarding superstars: Steve Caballero, Tony Hawk, and Rodney Mullen—an exceptionally gifted teen who was always coming up with new tricks. The third key to Powell Peralta's success was their use of video. Although it had become increasingly common among riders to film their performances, it was ultimately Powell Peralta who produced the first blockbuster skateboarding VHS tapes. *The Bones Brigade Video Show* and *Future Primitive* were released in rapid succession, opening eyes and blowing minds around the world.

There were cult brands and cult videos—all that was missing were magazines. Launched in 1981 and 1983, respectively, *Thrasher* and *Transworld* made skateboarding even more popular by inundating fans with new images on a monthly basis.

The 1980s witnessed a huge leap forward: the emergence of the first truly successful brands, the first cult magazines, and the first stars who brought skateboarding from the underground into the spotlight.

The 1980s:

Skateboarding Goes Pop

This decade was also a period of economic growth; for the first time, it was possible to make a decent living from skateboarding. In 1984, the Vision Street Wear brand invented the concept of the pro model, which enabled riders to get paid for every sale of a deck featuring their name on the underside.

Across the pond, things were happening in Europe, too. German skateboarder and businessman Titus Dittmann created his own distribution company and flooded the continent with American brands. He also created the Münster Monster Mastership, one of the largest contests of the 1980s. But he wasn't the only European with skateboarding on his mind. Pierre-André Senizergues, a young computer science student living in the suburbs of Paris, decided to drop everything and try his luck in California. Propelled onto the pro circuit, he became freestyle world champion at the age of twenty-two and, shortly after, secured the post of director of the American branch of shoe brand Etnies. Much as Vision had done for decks, Etnies commercialized the first pro model skate shoes—the Natas, a signature pair designed for rider Natas Kaupas.

Skateboarding also entered the wider pop culture during this period. The film *Thrashin'*, released in theaters in 1986, cast movie stars alongside skateboarding celebrities. In 1987, the band Suicidal Tendencies created the music genre Skate Punk, exemplified by their most well-known song, *Possessed to Skate*. In late 1989, audiences were introduced to two of the most famous skateboards in pop culture: Marty McFly's floating, futuristic deck in *Back to the Future Part II*, and the colorful board ridden by Bart Simpson.

The history of skateboarding has been defined by a series of upheavals, and the next revolution was already underway. This time, though, the action was happening in San Francisco, not Los Angeles. There, new riders were redefining the practice of skateboarding. Street skating was about to take over.

Guess What ? The 1980s may have been a game-changer for skateboarding, but this was also the decade that saw the majority of skateparks close. Insurance prices skyrocketed due to all the injuries sustained at the parks, forcing owners to shut them down.

Facing page   Steve Caballero at the Kona Skatepark, Florida, 1984. In the 1980s, skateboarding largely revolved around vert skating, and wearing protective gear (helmets, and elbow and knee pads) was common practice. Riders gradually abandoned this equipment as they ventured out into the streets.

Right   Josh Brolin during the filming of *Thrashin'*, 1986.

40

The 1990s: The Golden Age of Street Skating

In the 1990s, street skateboarding became more popular than vert. Riders abandoned ramps and skateparks in search of new challenges in the urban landscape. The practice of skateboarding changed once again, becoming more transgressive and more technical.

Facing page   Group of skaters
in Sydney, 1994.

Right   Harold Hunter
(right), member of the
Zoo York team, in New York.

Even today, the bricks that line the Embarcadero Plaza in San Francisco are riddled with odd pockmarks. While most visitors have no idea how they got there, skateboarding purists know the indentations were made by the trucks of riders who turned street skating into an art. Each mark was left by one of the local skateboarding greats, perhaps even the greatest of them all: Mike Carroll.

Carroll grew up in the San Francisco Bay Area, where he learned to skate with a group of friends and his brother Gregg. The young man spent most of his time on the Embarcadero Plaza, where he developed a complex and creative style that combined flips, grinds, and manuals. He eventually caught the attention of Mike Ternasky, one of the founders of the new, cool brand Plan B. At the time, Ternasky's ambition was to form the ultimate team, one that would bring together the best riders of the moment. He succeeded in convincing Carroll to join and, a year later, Plan B released *Questionable*—the video that would shape an entire generation of skaters. It depicted

a highly technical form of skateboarding, edited to a hip-hop soundtrack that contrasted with the more rock-influenced spirit of the 1980s. The video was an immediate success and incredibly influential. From that point on, street was king; riders deserted ramps and empty swimming pools in favor of the staircases and park benches downtown.

In response to this new discipline, skateboard decks became thinner and more maneuverable, and wheels grew smaller in diameter to reduce resistance during tricks. Riders adopted a new look, too: baggy pants—the bigger the better—were in style. It was known as the "big pants, small wheels" era.

Raised to stardom by the success of the *Questionable* video, Mike Carroll dreamed of creating his own company. In 1993, he teamed up with Canadian Rick Howard to create Girl Skateboards. When it came time to choose a logo for their brand, the two partners opted for—somewhat humorously— the symbol for the women's restroom.

This attention to detail quickly became the norm. In the second half of the decade, skateboarding grew more precise and refined.

The 1990s also witnessed a diversification within skateboarding. Although Girl and its team set the tone, other brands and cities left their mark on the decade. Alien Workshop and Toy Machine were two brands inspired by experimental film and contemporary art, and Zoo York flew the flag for New York skateboarding. Philadelphia also became a skateboarding stronghold, thanks in particular to the riders who hung out at the Love Park spot. The European scene was shaping up, too, led by the English brand Flip and the French brand Cliché.

Finally, the decade witnessed two crucial events. The X Games—the mega-contest that brought together every extreme sport in a single event—made its television debut. And then, in 1994, a humble skate shop in New York that would later become a fashion empire opened its doors: Supreme.

They were no joke, though; Girl Skateboards were dead serious. Carroll and Howard surrounded themselves with the cream of street skaters and produced their first video, titled *Goldfish*, codirected with filmmaker Spike Jonze. This trial run was popular with fans, but the brand's true masterpiece came out two years later, in 1996. Entitled *Mouse*, Girl's second video pushed skateboarding to a whole new level of perfection. Meticulously executed tricks became a total obsession: each jump had to soar, each landing had to be controlled, and no part of the rider, not even a fingertip, could touch the ground.

Above   Baggy pants, a distinctive fashion staple of skaters in the 1990s.

Right   The famous Love Park spot in Philadelphia—a street skating landmark.

Guess What ? Not everyone was happy about the development of street skating. Local governments complained about problems caused by skaters, such as noise and damage to urban structures, and installed skate-stoppers at popular spots. These small metal objects were intended to prevent riders from grinding on their favorite obstacles.

From the 2000s:

More than fifty years after it first appeared, skateboarding is still as appealing as ever. The proliferation of brands and the emergence of new riders around the world has led to a wealth of fresh styles and approaches.

The decades leading up to the 2000s were each dominated by a singular movement, but the early aughts ushered in an era defined by branching influences. An incredible number of brands have emerged in the last quarter-century, each with its own design, look, and approach to skateboarding. Radically opposed visions now coexist, from the hard-rock-inspired Zero, a brand whose team demonstrates an extreme, raw technique, to DGK, which draws on hip-hop codes and has adopted a more controlled way of skating, exuding attitude. At one point, these two conflicting approaches went head-to-head in the form of battles between hesh (rock-influenced) and fresh (rap-influenced) riders. Today, boundaries between styles are more fluid and the feuds are over.

As far as skateboarding disciplines are concerned, vert skating has made a comeback and is now on a level playing field with street skating; many riders even combine both techniques.

Finally, the supremacy of American riders has been overthrown by flourishing talent from around the globe. Over the years, many legendary skaters have left their mark on the sport's history: Tom Penny and Geoff Rowley from the UK, Arto Saari from Finland, and, more recently, Brazilian Letícia Bufoni and Yuto Horigome from Japan.

Today, skateboarding remains as fascinating as ever, and its continued appeal lies in the sport's openness, vibrancy, and capacity for reinvention.

Left   Nora Vasconcellos specializes in vert skating, but she's just as comfortable riding the street.

Facing page   Whether performing tricks in the skatepark or on urban fixtures, displaying technical precision or a rough and ready style, Louie Lopez is the ultimate versatile skater.

Something for Everyone

The Who

of
Skateb

's Who

Skateboarding is as much about those who make the boards as those who ride them. While brands continuously reimagine their gear and design iconic products, riders keep inventing increasingly jaw-dropping tricks that push the limits of complexity and daring. Let's take a look at the legendary brands and individuals who have forged the sport's reputation.

oarding

Vans started out as a typical family-owned company. In 1966, two brothers, Paul and Jim Van Doren, teamed up to create the Van Doren Rubber Company. They began by making deck shoes in their Anaheim workshop. It was a small-scale operation at first: each pair cost between two and five dollars, and was made and sold to order, onsite. Paul, who worked the register, would sometimes ask customers to come back the next day to pick up their purchases. But that didn't stop the Van Doren Shoe Company from quickly building an excellent reputation; customers praised the brand for its durable shoes and even gave them a nickname: Vans.

Rumors about a flexible and practically indestructible shoe spread along the California coast, eventually reaching the ears of skateboarders. In the early 1970s, Mark Van Doren, son of one of the Vans founders, told his father about skaters' enthusiasm for the brand's shoes. The Van Doren family decided to team up with Tony Alva and Stacy Peralta—two of skateboarding's rising stars—to create a model specifically for riders. The result was the #95, featuring a reinforced collar and the brand's signature waffle sole, which still lines Vans shoes today. A few months later,

Vans: The Ultimate Skate Shoe

When you think of skateboarding, the Vans logo is one of the first things that comes to mind. Since its early days, the brand has embraced the sport, becoming the epitome of West Coast cool in the process. More than just a skate shoe, Vans is a symbol of the California dream.

a second model designed for skateboarding was released: the #36 (now known as the Old Skool) was the first shoe to feature the brand's distinctive "jazz stripe" running along the side. It was an immediate hit; riders

Above   Skater wearing the Vans Sk8-Hi model, adorned with the brand's famous checkerboard motif.

Facing page   Roman Pabich, member of the Vans team.

around the world adopted Vans, making it the very first skate shoe brand.

In the 1980s, competition ramped up. Many other brands emerged and, as skating styles changed, consumers began to favor high-top models that provided more protective ankle support. In response to the trend, Vans designed a shoe for skateboarding star Steve Caballero. But it seems the brand went too far: the Cab, as it was called, definitely offered more protection, but its pronounced collar and tongue restricted movement. Street skaters in particular found the shoe too rigid, so they started cutting away the upper portion to get mobility back. When Vans found out what skaters were doing, they went back to the drawing board. In 1993, they released a lower version of the Cab that resembled the original model, but with a collar half as tall. Unsurprisingly, the new style was called the Half Cab. More than thirty years later, the model is still one of the most worn and appreciated by riders.

Today, Vans continues to ride the wave of popularity sparked by its iconic models, while still pursuing its innovative path. One of the brand's more recent achievements is the Lizzie—a pro model developed with skater Lizzie Armanto, which features an insole made from recycled materials. Vans has now transcended the world of skateboarding to become one of the most desirable sneaker brands in the world.

Guess What ? Who isn't familiar with Vans's famous "Off the Wall" slogan? It was invented in 1976, inspired by a phrase coined by the coolest riders to describe a particularly successful trick performed in an empty swimming pool.

Santa Cruz:

This Californian brand, founded in the 1970s, has stayed relevant over the decades by remaining technically and artistically innovative.

In 1973, in Santa Cruz, three friends with a passion for surfing (Richard Novak, Doug Haut, and Jay Shuirman) created a brand together, which they named by combining the first letters of their surnames: NHS. They started out producing and selling surfboards but couldn't make ends meet. The trio was beginning to question the future of their company when they received an order for 500 skateboards. In an effort to cut costs, they decided to make the decks from leftover fiberglass they had in the surfboard workshop. The durable, flexible boards were a hit with riders, and were so successful that the three partners decided to change tack: the result was Santa Cruz Skateboards.

The brand has stayed true to this spirit of innovation throughout its existence, starting in 1974 with the development of polyurethane Road Rider wheels equipped with precision bearings: the year after they were released, the company sold more than six million units. In the 1980s, Santa Cruz was also the first brand to design decks with a raised nose and

55

concave shape, vastly increasing the number of possible tricks. In 1994, the company tried to revolutionize the skateboard market with NuWood: a new plastic material it had developed that was supposed to make decks practically indestructible. Even better, used boards could be returned to be recycled into new decks. Unfortunately, skaters around the world remained loyal to their wooden decks, and NuWood was one of Santa Cruz's first commercial failures.

But the brand is popular for more than just its hardware. Part of Santa Cruz's appeal lies in its famous screaming hand logo, designed by artist Jim Phillips in 1985. The blue hand, which looks like something out of a comic book, is now worn around the world, on T-shirts, hoodies, caps, and more. This strong visual identity has also led to numerous collaborations with pop culture heavyweights: from Star Wars to Marvel comics to the Simpsons, the biggest names in entertainment have partnered with Santa Cruz, making it that much more of an icon.

Guess What ?

Santa Cruz has continually been in operation since its creation in 1973, making it the oldest skateboard brand in history!

Facing page   The screaming hand, Santa Cruz's emblematic logo.

Below   One of the first Santa Cruz skateboards, created in the 1970s.

The Innovator

Left Skater Mark Gonzales, founder of Blind.

Facing page Deck featuring the distinctive grim reaper mascot used by Blind since the 1990s.

After a bold start, Blind gradually lost ground due to increasingly fierce competition. It nevertheless remains one of the most important brands in the history of skateboarding.

Blind's name was born out of a joke. In 1988, rider Mark Gonzales—a member of Vision's team—decided to go his own way. He partnered with businessman Steve Rocco to create his brand. When it came to choosing a name, he settled on a gibe directed at his former sponsor. Since he had left Vision, his company would be called (you guessed it) Blind.

Gonzales's reputation and influence attracted a number of talented skateboarders; by 1989, many of the era's best riders had joined the Blind team, including Jason Lee, Rudy Johnson, Guy Mariano, and Danny Way. They were all ready to ditch their sponsors to join the rising brand. Two years later, Blind caught people's attention with the release of *Video Days*, still considered one of the most influential skateboarding videos of all time. The director—a young filmmaker enamored with the sport—would later become one of Hollywood's biggest names: Spike Jonze. He gave *Video Days* a cinematic touch with

Blind: Faded

a memorable opening sequence, skits performed by riders themselves, and a carefully curated soundtrack. It was perfect for showcasing the dynamic, technical, and creative style practiced by the members of the Blind team. Skateboarding fans around the world loved it, but this didn't stop many of the skaters who had signed a contract with the brand from leaving for other sponsors. After getting the better of its competitors, Blind now watched as other labels swiped its riders. New recruits stepped in to fill the void. One of them was Ronnie Creager, a true skateboarding magician capable of the most complex combinations. He would be the face of Blind for many years.

The brand's mascot—a mischievous grim reaper that appeared on decks and clothing—was another key to its success. The cartoon style was particularly appealing to teens, who would ask around at all the skate shops to find out if they sold the "brand with the skull." This image helped Blind sell a whole lot of skateboarding gear, as well as jeans and other products.

In the 2000s, other brands gradually outpaced Blind. Many talented riders have joined its team, but few stay very long. Although it's no longer at the top, Blind can still be proud of its influential legacy and now-iconic visual identity.

 Like Blind with its grim reaper, another brand became well known in the 1990s and 2000s for its cartoon mascots: World Industries, which depicted an elaborate rivalry between Flameboy, a flame, and Wet Willy, a drop of water. The two frenemies could be found burning, drowning, and otherwise harassing each other in a variety of comical situations on the brand's products.

Glory

Independ

Along with the deck and wheels, trucks are an essential component of any skateboard. While there are many brands that produce them, none is as popular as Independent, which still dominates the market nearly fifty years after its inception.

Independent was started by Richard Novak and Jay Shuirman, two of the Santa Cruz cofounders. Always looking to invent new things, they turned their attention to trucks. In the late 1970s, these metallic parts that attach the wheels to the deck were of very poor quality. Rick Blackhart, a professional rider at the time, complained that "[o]ut of the two major truck companies, one broke and one didn't turn." The challenges to be overcome were clear: durability along with maneuverability were what was needed.

In 1978, Novak and Shuirman teamed up with skater Fausto Vitello and designer Eric Swenson to create the Independent Stage 1s, intended to be the perfect trucks. They featured flexible construction and a metal base, at a time when some competitors were still using plastic. Rider Steve Olson didn't mince his words when he presented the Stage 1 trucks in *SkateBoarder* magazine: "They're f****** hot!" His words set the tone for Independent's rowdy and irreverent marketing approach, inspired by the rebellious spirit of California's biker scene. The brand was just as blunt in its approach to recruiting a team: Fausto Vitello went to skateboarding contests and handed out trucks wrapped in hundred-dollar bills to riders he thought had potential. In any case, Independent products were of such high quality that most of the best skaters were jockeying to get their sponsorship. Since there was less competition among truck makers than skateboard and shoe brands, Independent entered the 1980s with a near-monopoly on the market. Other manufacturers like Venture and Ace would eventually carve out a place for themselves, but even today Independent continues to assert its superiority.

dent: Screaming Metal

Guess What ?

True to its nonconformist spirit, Independent regularly posts *Build to Grind* videos on its YouTube channel, which teach viewers how to construct their own DIY skateboarding obstacles in the street using cement.

Facing page Aurélien Giraud, member of the Independent team.

Above Wrongly associated with military imagery, the cross in the Independent logo was gradually abandoned by the brand.

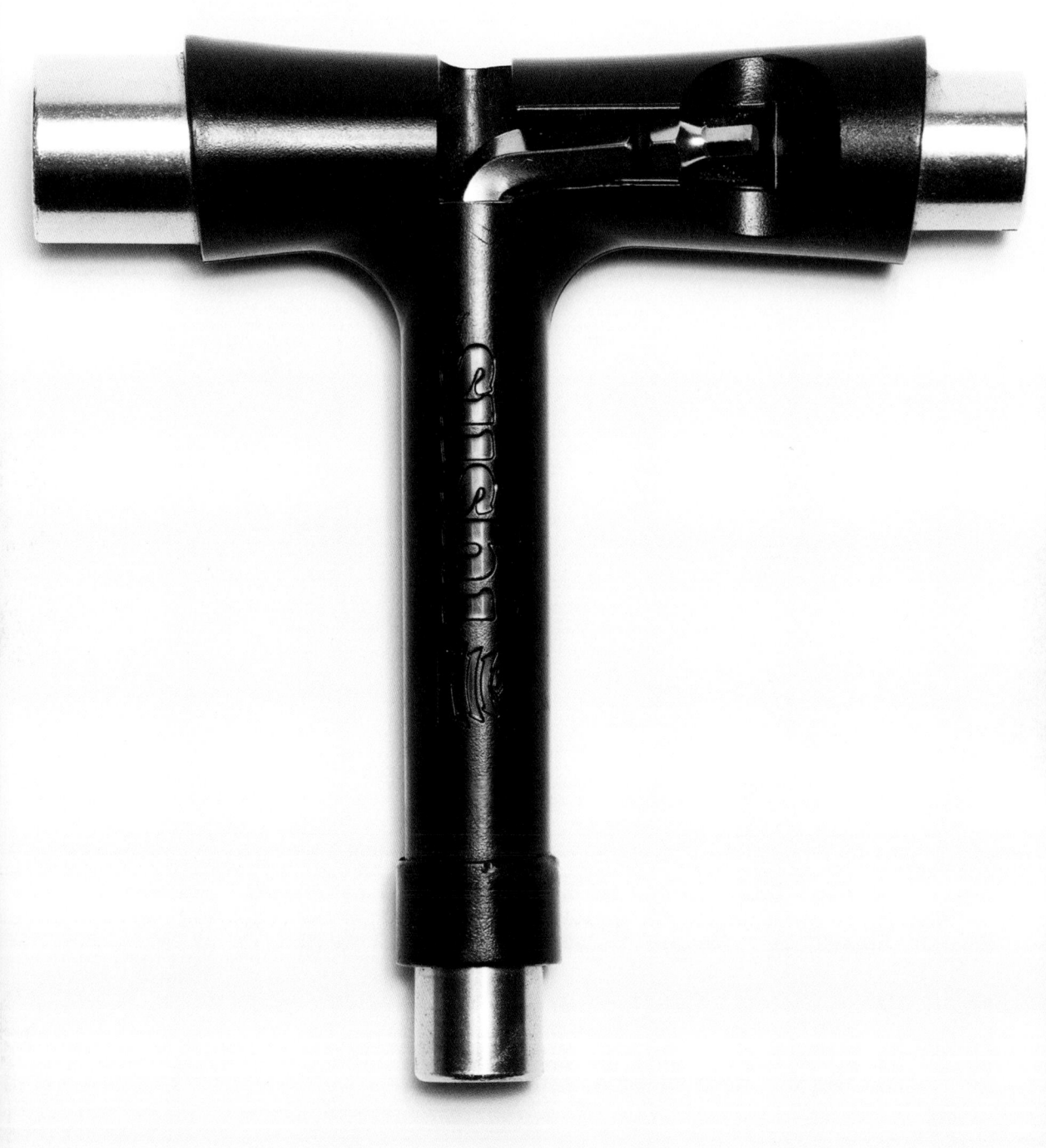

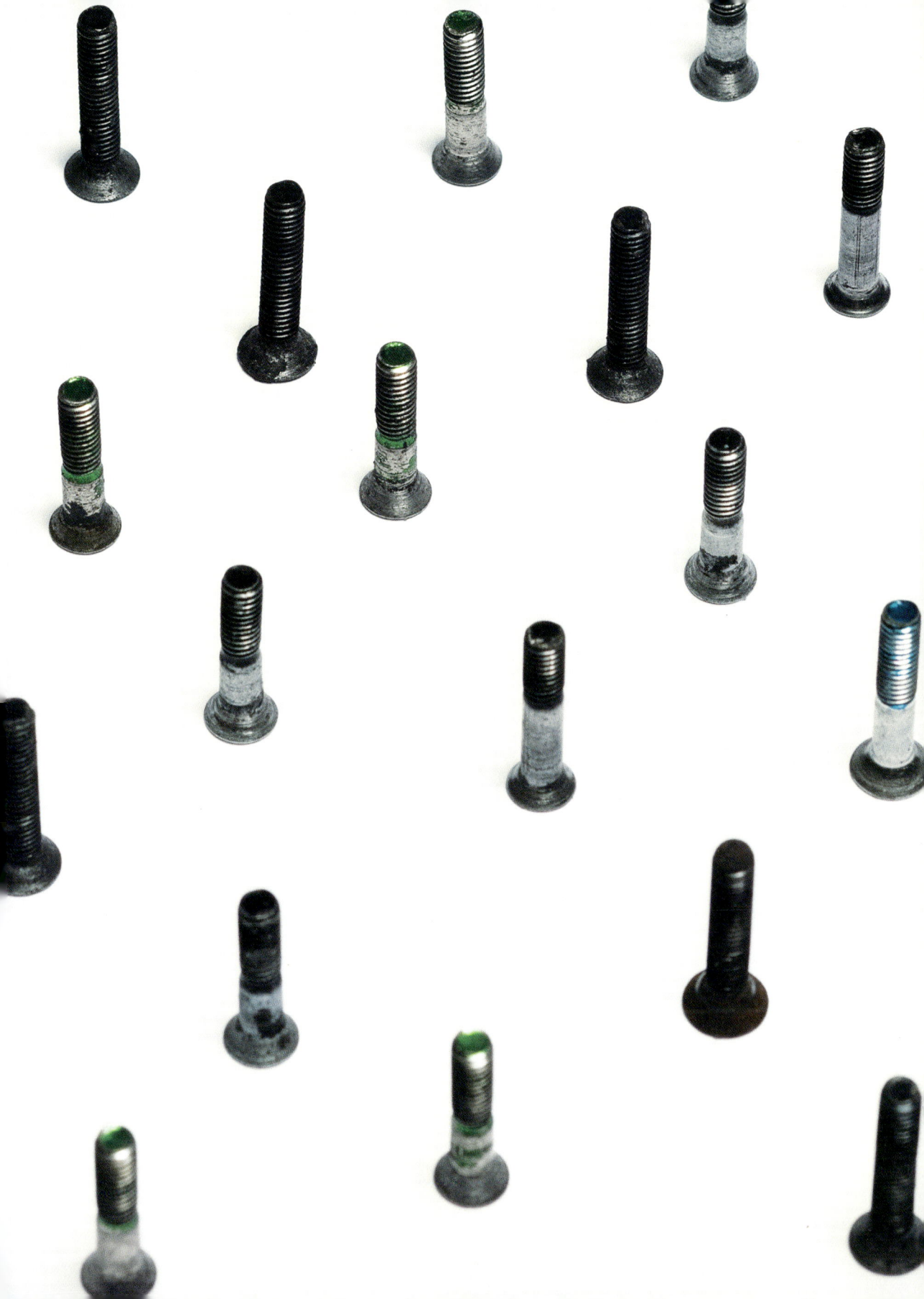

Spitfire:

More than just a piece of gear, Spitfire wheels have become an instantly recognizable sign of authenticity for riders. At skate spots around the world, riders praise them for being sturdy, grippy—and loud.

It's a familiar scene: a skater races down the middle of a steep street, wheels rumbling as they pick up speed, then squealing as they slide to a stop. By the sound alone, you can bet they're Spitfire wheels.

Created in 1987 by Jim Thiebaud, Spitfire began with a clear objective: to challenge the dominance of Bones Wheels, founded a few years earlier by Powell Peralta. To do so, Thiebaud and his teams developed their own urethane mixture called Formula Four. With this special material, they were able to make a wild but compelling promise to riders: no more flat spots. Flat spots are patches of wear and tear on a wheel that gradually compromise the wheel's roundness, sometimes making it completely flat in places. They can lead to reduced speed, unwanted vibrations, and a characteristic clicking sound. A very pronounced flat spot may be cause for replacing the wheel altogether.

Spitfire wheels quickly earned a reputation for their all-new formula. They were said to be nearly impossible to flatten, and they came in many different sizes and shapes ("classic," "conical," "radial," "tablet," etc.), meaning every rider could find the perfect model.

Beyond performance criteria, several less rational reasons make Spitfires the wheels of choice for many riders today. One is the brand's logo, created by artist Kevin Ancell, which features a demon's head surrounded by flames, suggesting fiendish speeds. Then there's the fact that Spitfire wheels are slightly yellower in color than wheels made by other brands. Considered off-putting at first, this characteristic color makes Spitfires instantly identifiable, adding to their popularity. And finally, there's the unmistakable sound they make; while many people find the rumble of Spitfires on asphalt irritating, it's music to a skater's ears.

Wheels o

SPITFIRE

Facing page   Spitfire wheels featuring the brand's unmistakable logo.

Below   Rider Shane O'Neill's board, equipped with Spitfire wheels.

Guess What ?

Powell Peralta and Spitfire recently entered a new race to innovate. Both brands attempted to create a wheel that is softer (and therefore more comfortable), while maintaining other qualities. Powell Peralta made the first move with the release of its Dragon Wheels, while Spitfire retaliated with its 93 Formula.

f Fortune

Throughout its existence, Girl has aimed for complete perfection and has succeeded most of the time—except when bad luck got in the way.

It all began in 1993. Mike Carroll, a skater idolized for his talent and instantly recognizable style, set out to create his own brand, partnering with Rick Howard, a Canadian rider who had moved to California. Frustrated by the unscrupulous practices of their previous sponsors, the two friends wanted to do things differently; their company would be built by skaters, for skaters. Most importantly, it would maintain a sense of fair play at all times.

But not everyone was happy about this development. Steve Rocco, one of the owners of the brand Plan B, the then sponsors of Carroll and Howard, got wind of their plans. He threatened legal action and went as far as demanding that skateboard manufacturers decline to make boards for Girl. Luckily, the rest of the skateboarding industry looked kindly on the newcomer, and enthusiasm for their venture grew quickly.

Girl: Top of the Class

So, Girl was able to form a team—and what a team it was. In the early years, the new brand attracted skateboarding's finest, including Jovontae Turner, Guy Mariano, Eric Koston, and Rick McCrank. The most gifted, most graceful riders signed up. Girl was so successful that, in 1994, Carroll and Howard had to create a second brand in order to sponsor all their recruits. The result was Chocolate Skateboards, which also signed incredibly talented riders like Keenan Milton and Gino Iannucci.

Their universe kept expanding with the addition of a truck brand (Royal) and a shoe brand (Lakai). The goal of these companies was to secure riders a future after their skateboarding career was over by

Above   Skater Mike Carroll's pro model deck by Girl.

Facing page   The Girl logo, which hasn't changed since the 1990s, is instantly recognizable.

employing them in the fields of design, management, distribution, etc.

The Girl empire became known for its increasingly ethical approach.

The brand's desire to do things right also came across in its videos. Ty Evans, Girl's official videographer, encouraged skaters to push themselves to deliver even more impressive images. Direction and editing were entrusted to big names, including Spike Jonze, whose *Yeah Right!*, released in 2003, is considered a masterpiece. Special effects, a green screen, slow motion, and cameos by celebrities such as Owen Wilson—this video has it all.

Another remarkable skill of Girl's founders was spotting and attracting young talent. In the early 2000s, as the original team began to age, Carroll and Howard, with help from their team manager, Sam Smyth, found rising stars Brandon Biebel, Jereme Rogers, Paul Rodriguez, Sean Malto, Mike Mo Capaldi, and Alex Olson. The future appeared to be in safe hands.

Guess What? Girl may have led the pack in most domains, but it fell short when it came to the inclusion of female skaters. Despite its name, the brand didn't sponsor women riders until 2019, when it signed Canadian Breana Geering.

Unfortunately, the brand and its new protégés suffered a run of bad luck. Several of the riders sustained serious injuries that significantly slowed their careers. Others decided to change sponsors, while others still completely lost interest in skating. But Girl managed to pick itself up after this rough patch.

Today, the brand is experiencing a resurgence driven by a new generation of riders (including Tyler Pacheco, Simon Bannerot, and Griffin Gass) and is enjoying renewed interest among younger skaters. Girl—the brand that always strives to do the right thing—has a bright future ahead.

Flip and Cliché:
Euro Style

While most of skateboarding's iconic brands hail from the States, Europe has produced some important names of its own. Among the most remarkable are Flip and Cliché. Although both were created in Europe, they have each followed their own, very different path.

For once, the story begins far from the sunny beaches of California. In 1987, three young skaters from London—Graham McEachran, Jeremy Fox, and Duncan Houlton—decided to create their own brand, which they called Deathbox. To round out their team, they recruited four other riders: Tom Penny, Andy Scott, Danish rider Rune Glifberg, and a teen from Liverpool named Geoff Rowley. Shortly after, Deathbox released its first video and became a sensation in the UK. Success seemed within easy reach, but there was just one problem: England and its weather are not particularly well suited to skateboarding. Incessant rain and cobblestone streets slowed progress for the Deathbox crew, who dreamed of smooth sidewalks that were always dry. In 1994, they made the decision to relocate the brand to California, changing its name in the process. From then on, it was known as Flip.

On the sunny West Coast, Flip's core crew made noticeable progress. Glifberg won many contests, Penny developed a nonchalant style that fascinated aficionados, and Rowley proved to be one of the most talented skaters of his generation. Over the years, other gifted riders joined the brand's ranks, including Arto Saari, Bastien Salabanzi, Mark Appleyard, and Ali Boulala. These riders of different nationalities, influenced by diverse styles, made Flip's team one of the most eclectic around. This collection of talents exploded onto the scene in 2002 in the video *Sorry*—the title reads like an apology for the shock it delivers. The video rocketed Flip to the top of the global skateboarding scene. Not bad for a bunch of dreamy London kids.

Now let's rewind a few years. Back when Flip was still called Deathbox, its riders included Jérémie Daclin, a young man from Lyon. It was important to Daclin to ride for a European brand, so he was disappointed by his sponsor's choice to move to the US. He decided to stay in France and create his own brand with the slogan "Euro Skate Co" and a logo based on the map of Europe. The name reflected Daclin's love of photography; Cliché is the French word for snapshot.

This desire to see the emergence of a European, or even French, skateboarding culture was conveyed in video titles like *Europa*, *Bon Appétit*, and *Freedom Fries*. Fred Mortagne, a photographer and videographer known for his refined compositions, produced the brand's videos.

Over the years, Cliché has sponsored many European skaters, some of whom later left to make their way in the US. In 2005, the brand recruited its first American rider: Joey Brezinski.

After being acquired by the Salomon group, Cliché was sold in 2009 to Dwindle Distribution before ceasing operations in 2016. Since then, Daclin has created a new brand, Into The Wild, and regularly publishes Instagram posts of himself doing tricks on the banks of the Rhône—a Lyon guy through and through!

Facing page Skater Roland Gueissaz's pro model deck by Cliché, from 1997.

Below, top Jérémie Daclin, founder of Cliché.

Below, bottom Rune Glifberg at a contest in Costa Mesa, California, in 2010.

Although they share common roots, éS and Emerica have each developed a distinct identity, demonstrating the diversity within the skateboarding culture.

To understand how these two brands came to be, we have to go back to 1986, when the French company Rautureau Apple released a line of skate shoes called Etnics; the name was quickly modified to Etnies following a lawsuit brought by the Etonic brand. To promote itself, Etnies sponsored a young French rider, Pierre-André Senizergues, who relocated to the US, where he attracted attention with his skateboarding talent. At the same time, he began his business career as manager of Etnies's American branch.

In 1995, things got complicated. Rautureau Apple changed hands, and the future of Etnies was uncertain. So, Senizergues decided to create his own subsidiary, which he called Etnies America, later shortened to

Emerica. At the same time, he teamed up with rider Don Brown to create éS, another skate shoe brand with a higher-end, athletic look. The following year, he managed to buy Etnies and found himself at the head of three brands at once. It was time to give each one its own identity.

Etnies would be the most neutral, with mainstream appeal. The most technical would be éS, with models inspired by high-performance footwear and equipped with features like air cushions, padded collars, and colorways borrowed from basketball teams. Emerica was the wild child; its models

éS and Emerica: Heads and Tails

featured darker colors, an angular logo, and narrower silhouettes that were ideal for pairing with ripped slim-fit jeans. It followed that the éS and Emerica teams would be polar opposites, represented by technical skaters in baggy pants at éS and daredevils with rockstar attitude at Emerica.

Even today, these two very different sibling companies continue to follow their respective paths—never identical but always complementary. It's up to each rider to choose their favorite.

Facing page   Pierre-André Senizergues, cofounder of the éS and Emerica brands and executive producer of *The 11th Hour*, Leonardo DiCaprio's documentary on climate change.

Below   The Emerica logo, in the brand's characteristic green hue.

Guess What ?

In addition to its logo and shoe design, Emerica has been known for using the color green in its branding for decades. In 2020, the brand even released a video called, quite simply, *Green*.

GO
SKATEBOARDING
Emerica.
2000 (F) CVC

blonde

Baker:

While skateboarding is generally considered an extreme sport, no other brand takes on this mantle more than Baker. Rowdy and outrageous—and known to go too far at times—Baker continues to make waves in the world of skateboarding.

Baker's story is closely tied to that of its founder, skater Andrew Reynolds. After leaving his native Florida for California, he was soon noticed for his innate talent and joined the Birdhouse team, first as an amateur skater, then as a professional in 1995. He had no family in the area, so he lived with other young riders in an apartment on Warner Avenue, in Los Angeles. Left to their own devices, the crew lived life in the fast lane, splitting their time between skate sessions and alcohol-fueled parties.

In 2000, Reynolds wanted to strike out on his own. He dreamed of creating a brand that would embody his edgy lifestyle and put his party-loving friends in the spotlight. With the help of videographer Jay Strickland, he released the video *Baker Bootleg*, which included tricks and shots deemed unusable by Birdhouse. Shortly after, he legitimized Baker's existence with a second video, *Baker2G*. Besides the usual tricks, it was full of more or less tasteful jokes, including prank calls, insults, and altercations with passersby. Some scenes were actually cut during editing, after Baker was threatened with legal action. Magazine ads for the brand ran in the same vein: they showed riders picking fights with people on the street and recounting their stints in rehab. This trashy, hedonistic tone was appealing and sent Baker's popularity skyrocketing.

But by pushing the limits as far as they could go, the Baker Boys, as they were known, eventually got burned. Several members of the team suffered various addictions, and it showed in their performance on the board. The brand's young recruits also found themselves confronted with all manner of excess, and it wasn't uncommon to see teens

The Enfar

sponsored by Baker knocking back beer after beer. Kevin "Spanky" Long's trajectory perfectly demonstrates the old Baker culture: heralded as a future prodigy when he joined Baker in 2003, he then went through a long substance-fueled slump before making a triumphant return in the late 2010s. Baker even celebrated his sobriety in an ad.

One by one, the team's riders followed his example, and the 2019 video *Baker 4* features nearly the whole team reunited, projecting renewed health and focus. During several poignant scenes, Reynolds can be seen skating alongside his daughter Stella. It looks like the bad boys of Warner Avenue have grown up.

Facing page   Decks featuring the Baker logo—a classic model that the brand reissues year after year.

Below   Andrew Reynolds, founder of Baker.

Guess What ?

Despite its rebellious side, Baker nearly found itself at the center of a television reality show. *I Wanna Be a Baker* was an elimination-style talent show for skateboarding, where competitors would have to perform a series of tricks to win a sponsorship deal with the brand. A pilot was filmed but was never broadcast.

nt Terrible

Dark, harsh, uncompromising: Zero is for skaters who are willing to risk it all. No matter how many stairs they have to jump or how far they have to drop, riders who flaunt the infamous skull fear nothing.

Never had a failed trick been so influential. One day in 1997, a young skater tried something outrageous: in a San Diego schoolyard, he ollied over a handrail, performed a melon grab, and landed nearly twenty feet (six meters) below. As he came down on his board, it split in two from the impact. He fell hard but picked himself up, unhurt. This moment in skateboarding history is known as the "leap of faith" and remains the sport's most glorious failure.
The man behind it was Jamie Thomas, the founder of Zero.

A year earlier, in response to what he called "the mediocrity in skateboarding during this time," Thomas had created Zero, a brand that would reflect his own skate practice: hair-raising, with an appetite for highly daring, even dangerous tricks. Naturally, he chose a skull for the logo and a slogan that reads like a challenge: "Dare to skate, dare to live." The deck art, featuring crucifixes, blood smears, and gothic type, looks like something from a heavy metal album cover.
Zero became the preferred brand of the boldest skaters, and Thomas gathered

Zero:
The Daredevil

a group of risktakers to form his team. In the early 2000s, he discovered a rare talent in Chris Cole, who was able to combine technical flair with sheer audacity. Cole would go on to represent Zero for many years.

But Thomas was more than an exceptional stuntman; he also had a knack for business. He grew the Zero brand and created another, for shoes, called Fallen Footwear. In 2006, Ernst & Young named him regional Entrepreneur of the Year—proof that you can skate like there's no tomorrow and still prepare for the future.

Guess What ?

If the Zero logo looks familiar, that's because it's almost identical to the skull stamped on the T-shirt worn by Sid, the troublesome pre-teen in the animated film *Toy Story*.

Facing page   A Zero deck.

Below   Chris Cole, member of the Zero team from 2004 to 2014.

The most desirable, the most exclusive, the most enigmatic— Supreme racks up the superlatives. Its products sell for a fortune, and its stores have endless lines outside. The brand has become such a sensation, it's easy to forget that Supreme started out just like any other skateboard brand—well, almost.

In 1994, a new skate shop opened on Lafayette Street, in New York. Like every other skate shop, this one sold decks, gear, and clothing. But upon closer inspection, one detail stood out. The logo on the door was inspired by the work of artist Barbara Kruger; a seven-letter word written in white Futura type on a red background: Supreme.

This (unauthorized) reference to the artist spoke volumes. It reflected the desire of James Jebbia, Supreme's founder, to embed his company within a cultural context that extended beyond skateboarding. Like an exhibition curator, he selected his favorite artists and artworks, and used his brand as a showcase. Over the years, Supreme has released clothing collections inspired by Martin Scorsese, Damien Hirst, and New Order,

Supre

me: The King of Hype

Guess What?

In 2019, the prestigious auction house Sotheby's put more than 1,300 Supreme products up for sale. A complete collection of skateboards released by the brand was sold for the modest sum of $800,000.

and even rereleased several Miles Davis albums. In doing so, Jebbia hopes to share his own tastes and preferences, while exposing crowds of young skaters to major works in various cultural fields.

Even better, Supreme pulled off the feat of being edifying without being irritating, thanks to a massive injection of cool. The store's first employees were popular neighborhood riders who had played extras in Larry Clark's film *Kids*. Supreme's regular collaborations gave it another incredible advantage; they included brands like Nike, Vans, Doc Martens, and Bape, as well as big names in luxury, and even furniture designers and a Japanese fly-fishing apparel company. Nothing was off limits. Supreme was a total brand that could slap its famous box logo on everything—and anything. The final ingredient in the company's secret sauce was a then unheard-of sales technique based on exclusivity and frustration: the drop. Each week, new products were released in limited quantities, stoking fans' desire.

Facing page   Over the years, Supreme has commissioned many renowned artists to illustrate its decks.

Above   The usual line outside the Supreme store in London.

"If we can sell 600, I make 400," said Jebbia in an interview.

Supreme was so successful that within several years, the brand became a heavy hitter in fashion, opening stores in cities around the world, including Los Angeles, San Francisco, Tokyo, Osaka, Paris, London, Milan, and Berlin. In 2017, Jebbia sold 50 percent of his shares in the company, and in 2020 Supreme was acquired for 1.5 billion dollars.

So, where does skateboarding fit in? Since its inception, Supreme has recruited dozens of talented and creative riders for its team—many of whom are also big personalities—from legends like Mark Gonzales and Harold Hunter to present-day celebrities like Rowan Zorilla and Tyshawn Jones. Their performances are compiled in distinctive videos directed by William Strobeck, the brand's official videographer. By remaining true to its roots, Supreme has been able to preserve its authenticity and legitimacy, and continues to inspire everyone from skateboarding purists to hype-addicts.

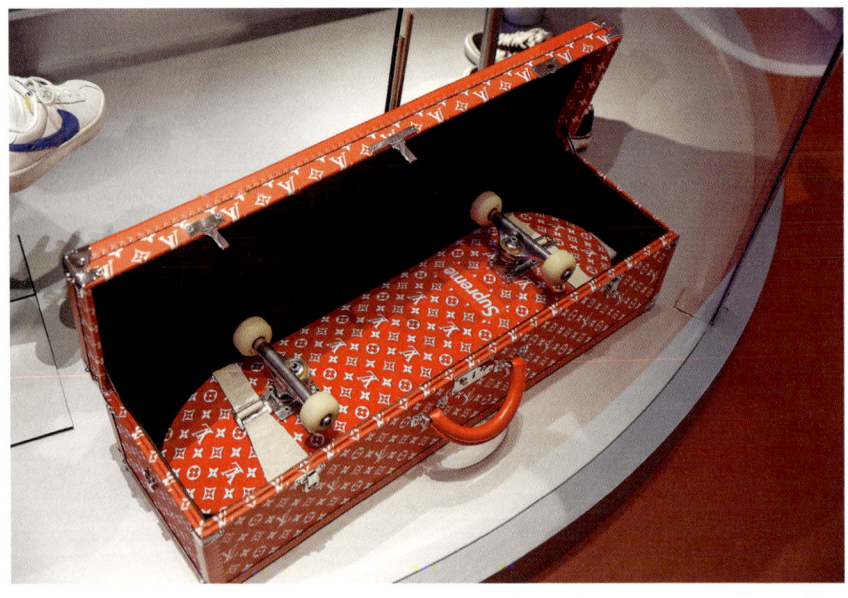

Above Supreme decks from the fall-winter 2024 collection.

Left Board and trunk from the 2017 collab between Supreme and Louis Vuitton.

New

New skateboarding brands are always springing up. Not a day goes by without another rider getting in on the game in the hopes of creating something unique, and maybe even becoming a future success story.

The most recent enterprises include New York-based Limosine Skateboards, defined by a visual identity inspired by the 2000s, along with unusual tricks performed on the most inhospitable obstacles and spots (brick walls, cobblestone streets, dirt paths).

Another brand, Quasi, makes use of strange visuals that combine collage and abstract art. Frog Skateboards takes a similar approach, although the brand has a more childlike aesthetic. Sci-Fi Fantasy, created by rider Jerry Hsu and informed by his love of photo and Internet culture, is another one to watch.

Newcomers also include rising empires. At least that's the path former pro skater and now entrepreneur-artist Jason Dill seems to be on. He manages two very successful brands, Fucking Awesome and Hockey. Even more ambitious is Swede Pontus Alv's endeavor, which combines a skateboard brand (Polar) with a shoe brand (Last Resort) and is starting to outshine industry heavyweights. The momentum shows no signs of stopping.

on the

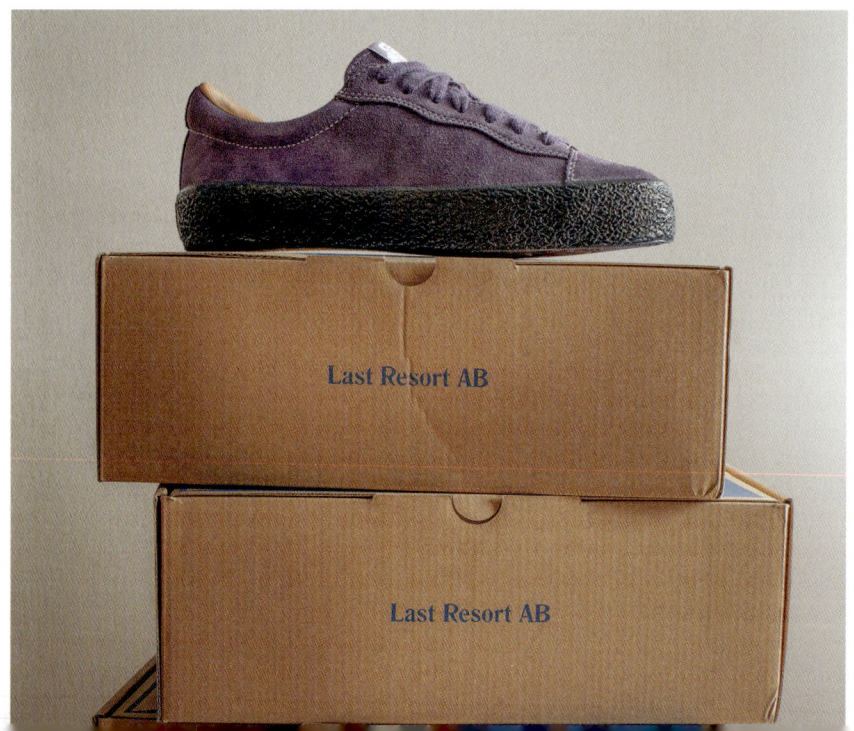

Last Resort AB

Last Resort AB

Scene

Enter

Protective of its counter-culture image, skateboarding has long regarded traditional sportswear brands with suspicion. To make inroads, large manufacturers have had to prove themselves and demonstrate that they understand and respect the particularities of this new market.

Spo

As soon as riders stopped skating barefoot, specialized shoe brands began to appear. In addition to the original brand Vans, there was Hang Ten, Hobie, Vision, and Airwalk. Other, more unexpected brands like tennis's Wilson and the French brand Palladium attempted to release models designed for skateboarding, but their efforts were short-lived. In the 1980s, many skaters repurposed basketball shoes and wore Nike Blazers, Converse Fastbreaks, and Adidas Forums, which had padded collars that protected riders' ankles.

This trend waned in the 1990s, when brands created by skaters for skaters flourished, and the supply grew so much that sportswear giants were driven out. Even worse, their attempts to break into the skateboarding market were perceived by most riders as opportunistic. In 1997, Nike was refused access to the skate shop distribution network, which didn't feel it needed the Swoosh to prosper.

Converse's more subtle approach, however, was relatively successful. The brand settled for sending shoes to popular riders and running a few ads that didn't even mention skateboarding (they were for Converse's line of basketball shoes) in *Thrasher* magazine.

In 2001, Nike tried again, this time adopting a Trojan horse strategy. The company began by acquiring Savier: an independent brand that had been created a year earlier,

orts Brands

Facing page and right Tyshawn Jones, a star rider for Adidas (facing page), and his pro model skate shoes (right).

and that used proprietary technologies like Zoom Air cushioning. Sales were moderate, but Nike had a goal beyond that; the company wanted to carve out a place in the market without being rejected, and in this sense, Savier was a success. Once skaters felt reassured, Nike could get down to business. In 2002, Nike SB was created. In 2004, the brand recruited rider Paul Rodriguez who for many years had been recognized for his talent on the board. Other big names quickly followed, including Lance Mountain, a cult figure of the 1980s who acted as something of a mentor to the team. Since then, Nike has been considered a skateboarding brand alongside all the others.

More sportswear heavyweights rushed to follow Nike's lead, including Adidas in 2006, New Balance in 2013, and Asics in 2023. Each time, the strategy has been the same: sponsor undisputed stars and bring in a group of promising young talent, along with a former skateboarding celebrity to act as a guide. And, most importantly, start things off quietly, without fanfare. Using this proven formula, traditional athletic brands have acquired a considerable part of the skate shoe market, often at the expense of the sport's pioneers, some of whom have been forced to throw in the towel.

Théo Monelli, cofounder of Bisous Skateboards

A committed rider since childhood, Théo Monelli has poured his knowledge of fashion into creating Bisous Skateboards: a modern and attractive brand whose style extends well beyond the skatepark.

How did the Bisous Skateboards project come about?

I started skateboarding when I was eleven. It was my first true passion, and deeply influenced my teenage years and the kind of music, fashion, and magazines I liked. Skateboarding culture drew me in immediately. At the same time, my studies and professional experiences revolved around clothing. I worked in a store that sold skateboard brands, and I thought that it would be amazing if, one day, I too could sell a T-shirt or a board with my logo on it. As for the name, my associate and I wanted something that sounded French and that would also appeal to girls, who I didn't feel were represented enough in skateboarding culture. We started with a T-shirt and a deck, because having your own board is every skater's dream. They sold well, so we made two decks and two T-shirts, then three, then five—and *voilà*!

Was it difficult to carve out a place among all the other brands?

Things went pretty smoothly, because I was lucky enough to have a good network. I was working as a buyer, so I was already familiar with the preorder, production, and distribution processes. I wasn't too worried, because I still had a job on the side. We forged ahead without overthinking things. Above all, we wanted to create a brand universe that we identified with. We started with a pop-up store, and right away we felt people's enthusiasm for our cultural references, whether they were related to skateboarding or not.

So, this extra cultural flair helped make Bisous a success?

We made a conscious choice not to be a diehard skateboard brand. We wanted there to be more fashion-oriented and feminine aspects as well. Our collaborations with skateboarding heavyweights like Element and DC Shoes give us a certain legitimacy, but we've also worked with the shoemaker Weston, as well as cosmetic brands. However, skateboarding remains the central theme of everything we produce, from our visuals to our collaborations.

How did you come to work with cosmetics brands?

When we started out, we were contacted by Violette Serrat, a renowned makeup artist and founder of Violette FR. She had bought one of our T-shirts in a store and found us on Instagram. She asked us to create a collection to accompany her line of beauty products. If I were a purist, I would have refused. But I've always enjoyed exploring areas that are new to me.

Who were your models when you created Bisous?

Our inspirations were Supreme, Palace, Stüssy—all those brands that have a strong lifestyle element. We're stoked about skateboarding, but it's also very cool to do other things as well.

How do you find a balance between this lifestyle dimension and maintaining credibility with skateboarders?

All of our collections and all of our communications have some connection to skateboarding. As a result of the Covid-19 pandemic and the increase in the price of raw materials, we only make boards for our marketing events, which are then available for purchase throughout the year. Now that things are pretty much back to normal, we're thinking about making boards on a more

regular basis. We're also putting together a team made up of skaters with different styles: not necessarily with performance in mind, but rather with the aim of cultivating a variety of approaches, like Baker did at one point. We're also looking for women skateboarders to bring more balance to the lineup.

Below   Bisous:
a brand that combines
skateboarding and lifestyle.

Legendary Riders

*A teeter-totter
on wheels is
the new fad
and menace*

That thing 19-year-old Pat Mc-Gee is balancing on is a skate-board, the most exhilarating and dangerous joy-riding device this side of the hot rod. A two-foot piece of wood or plastic mounted on wheels, it yields to the skill-ful user the excitements of skiing or surfing. To the unskilled it gives the effect of having stepped on a banana peel while dashing down the back stairs. It is also a menace to limb and even to life.

For decades youngsters have been nailing old skate wheels to boards and trying to ride them, but the skateboard took on its official name and epidemic proportions when surfing enthusiasts in California began making sophisticated versions about four years ago. The fever has swept east, scooping up everyone from matrons to mop-pets in its tooth-rattling wake. Boards cost from $1.98 to a mo-torized $50, and manufacturers predict sales of more than $30 million in 1965. Orthopedic special-ists may take in even more. Young adults like Miss McGee, who be-came a skateboarder after having been an avid surfer, seldom suffer more than loss of dignity, but less experienced folk get hurt. A Los Angeles hospital reports 25 skate-board cases a month, two thirds of them broken childish bones, and the toll will get worse as summer sends a horde of youthful skate-boarders out into the streets. In the past month two children have been killed in the east when they ca-reened into traffic on their boards.

SKATEBOARD MANIA

CONTINUED 128C

Patti McGee

Nationality	**Born**	**Nickname**
American	**1945**	**"First Betty"**
		("Betty" was the name given to the first women skateboarders in the 1960s)

Her story Patti McGee began
skateboarding in 1963, entirely by accident. At the time,
she was working in a sporting goods store, where she was
asked to give away a skateboard each evening. When the kid
who was supposed to do the skateboard demonstration
didn't show up one night, McGee was forced to step in
at the last moment. She did a few kick turns, and the crowd
was enchanted. Encouraged by this debut, she asked her
brother to make her a skateboard and progressed at lightning
speed; she won her first competition in 1964 and went
pro in 1965. The same year, she appeared on the cover
of *SkateBoarder* magazine and *Life*.

Her moment of glory In 2010, Patti McGee became
the first woman inducted into the Skateboarding Hall of Fame.

The Trailblazer

Natas Kaupas

Nationality	Born	Nickname
American	**1969**	**"Natas"**

His story   Born into a family of Lithuanian descent, Natas Kaupas grew up in Santa Monica. He began skating as a child but was reluctant to hang out in skateparks, as was common among other riders at the time. His playground was the street—the one and only. This radical choice unleashed his creativity: he rode walls and used elements of the urban landscape, such as benches, fences, and fire hydrants, as obstacles, taking freestyle tricks beyond the competition circuit. He rose to fame with his urban experiments; in 1984, he was photographed wallriding, which was, at that time, a totally new trick and landed him on the cover of *Thrasher* magazine. From this moment, his popularity surged. In 1986 he joined the Santa Cruz team and became its star rider. In 1991, he started his own brand, 101 Skateboards, and designed most of the visuals himself. Unfortunately, he sustained an ankle injury the following year that brought his illustrious career to an end. But he remained involved in many skateboarding-related projects, including the launch of *Big Brother* magazine.

His moment of glory   In the video *Streets on Fire*, released by Santa Cruz in 1989, Natas Kaupas performed a trick that left audiences speechless: he ollied up onto a fire hydrant and spun around on top of it, twice. This revolutionary trick is now known as the "Natas spin."

The High Priest of Street

Tony Hawk

Nationality	Born	Nickname
American	**1968**	**"The Birdman"**

His story

Tony Hawk was nine years old when he got on a skateboard for the first time. A hyperactive kid with a keen intelligence, he was encouraged by his parents to use skateboarding as an outlet, and he threw himself into it wholeheartedly. The results were almost immediate: he won trophy after trophy at contests and went pro at the age of fourteen. At seventeen, he boasted about making more money than his high school teachers. Besides his career as a rider, Hawk went into an entrepreneurial frenzy and started several projects. He created a skateboard brand (Birdhouse) and a clothing label (Hawk Clothing), and he teamed up with video game maker Activision to create the phenomenally successful *Tony Hawk's Pro Skater* franchise. This major foray into pop culture made Hawk a superstar—he's dubbed the Michael Jordan of skateboarding. In the early 2000s, after a final series of victories at the X Games, he retired from competition, but continued to set himself the wildest challenges: to skate a 360º spiral loop, to slide along a railing set on fire, and to jump between two skyscrapers. Even today, the Birdman continues to fly on his skateboard. He is also committed to promoting the sport and making it more accessible through his foundation, The Skatepark Project, which funds the construction of skateboarding infrastructure throughout the US.

His moment of glory

In 1999, Tony Hawk completed the first ever "900" (a 900º aerial rotation, or two and a half spins, on a ramp)—a feat many riders have attempted but few have succeeded in replicating.

The Superstar

Rodney Mullen and Daewon Song

Nationality	Born	Nicknames
American	**1966 and 1975**	**"Godfather of Skateboarding" and "Daewon"**

Their story Rodney Mullen's skateboarding career didn't get off to the best start. At first, his father forbade him from practicing the sport, which he thought was dangerous; he eventually gave in, on the condition that his son always wear protective gear. Not only that, young Mullen suffered from severe supination of the feet, which forced him to wear special shoes, even when he was sleeping. Despite these obstacles, he quickly proved himself to be a true skateboarding prodigy. He caught the attention of sponsors and began performing demonstrations around the US, achieving a level of fame that was unprecedented for a skateboarder. Gifted with unrivaled creativity and skill, he invented many tricks that have since become an essential part of the repertoire of any self-respecting rider. During one of his performances at a school, Mullen made a strong impression on a Korean American teen named Daewon Song, who also had an innate talent for skateboarding. What Song didn't know is that he had caught the eye of his idol. A few weeks later, Song received several decks from Mullen and was formally introduced to him. The two developed a deep friendship, and Song was quickly skating at the same level as his former role model. In 2003, Mullen and Song went from being just pals to being associates, too, when they created their brand, Almost Skateboards.

Facing page   Rodney Mullen (left) and Daewon Song (right).

Their moment of glory In 1997, to showcase their respective talents, the pair released the video *Rodney Mullen vs. Daewon Song*, which features the two buddies engaged in a friendly contest. It was so successful that two more "rounds" were subsequently filmed and released.

The Technical Wizards

Danny Way

Nationality
American

Born
1974

Nickname
**"Christ" or
"The Man
with Wings"**

His story   Danny Way had a difficult
childhood. His father died before his first birthday, and his
mother remarried a man who abused both her and her children.
As a kid, Way found an escape in skateboarding, especially
skating ramps, which gave him a thrilling sense of freedom.
He won his first vert competition at the age of fifteen and joined
the Powell Peralta team. Over time, he developed an increasingly
dramatic style of skating and specialized in high air and big air:
disciplines that involve taking off from the largest possible
ramps. In 2003, he had a new kind of obstacle built: the
megaramp. Skating this colossal structure enabled him to break
the world record for the highest air on a skateboard several
times over. Once he had surpassed this limit, no challenge
seemed impossible to him—including jumping from a helicopter
to land on a ramp and jumping over the Great Wall of China.
In 2015, at the age of forty-one, he even beat his own world
record for the biggest air off a quarter-pipe when he reached
a height of 25½ feet (7.77 meters), proving that his nicknames
"Christ" and "The Man with Wings" are well deserved.

His moment of glory   Danny Way is one of the
rare riders to have been named Skater of the Year twice
by *Thrasher* magazine.

The Superhero

Keith Hufnagel

Nationality	Born	Nickname
American	**1974**	**"Huf"**

His story　　　　Keith Hufnagel grew up in New York, far from California's perfect skate spots. He earned his stripes on the famous Brooklyn Banks, a series of sloping brick surfaces popular with skaters in the Big Apple. At the age of eighteen, he started college in San Francisco, but dropped out after six months to focus on skateboarding. Accustomed to the difficult terrain of New York streets, Hufnagel skated with strength, flying over the sidewalks of his new West Coast playground. This extraordinary style set him apart and endeared him to sponsors. In 1993, he began to skate professionally for Fun Skateboards, then joined Real a few years later. Hufnagel's other love was fashion, and in 2002 he opened a store called Huf, which sold a curated selection of clothing, skateboarding gear, and sneakers. Huf became a brand in its own right, earning a place alongside the giants of streetwear with its classic designs and irreverent tone, and Hufnagel was hailed as a key influence in skateboarding culture. But tragedy brought his stellar career to an abrupt end: in 2020, Hufnagel died from a brain tumor. His talent, his legendary style, and his enduringly successful brand remain his legacy.

Above　　Keith Hufnagel (left) and Cleon Peterson.

His moment of glory　　　　In 1997, Keith Hufnagel was featured on the cover of *Thrasher* magazine, which paid tribute to his incredible jumps with the headline "Biggest Air Ever."

Huf Forever

Eric Koston

Nationality	**Born**	**Nickname**
Thai American	**1975**	**"Froston"**

His story Eric Koston was born in Thailand, and his family moved to the US when he was just nine months old. At the age of eleven, he took up skateboarding, trying to copy his older brother. Unlike other riders, Koston confesses that he progressed slowly but surely, trying his best to avoid a bad fall. But that didn't stop him becoming a gifted and creative skater. Eddie Elguera, a well-known professional skater, took young Koston under his wing, giving him boards and getting him to participate in demonstrations and contests. Elguera also helped Koston to get his first sponsor, H-Street. This enabled Koston to meet other skaters who encouraged him to explore every discipline, from ramp to street skating. This training regimen made him an extremely versatile rider who didn't seem to have any shortcomings. In the mid-1990s, he was among the hottest names and was approached by many brands. In 1996, he joined Girl, where he stayed until 2015, becoming one of the brand's legendary skaters in the process. Koston's collaboration with éS shoes was another match made in heaven; in 1997, he designed the iconic Koston 1 with the brand. In 2007, he teamed up with rider Steve Berra to create the Berrics in Los Angeles, a huge skatepark where many videos were filmed and then posted on YouTube.

His moment of glory In 2009, Eric Koston—a huge fan of basketball and the Los Angeles Lakers in particular—had the opportunity to appear in an ad alongside NBA superstar Kobe Bryant, marking one of the first times a skater had been placed on the same level as a more mainstream, famous athlete.

The King of Versatility

Elissa Steamer

Nationality	**Born**	**Nickname**
American	**1975**	**"Gizmo"**

Her story Elissa Steamer grew up in Fort Myers, Florida. After a stint in BMX biking, she developed a passion for skateboarding, and it soon became clear that she was exceptionally talented. Everywhere she went, other riders had to acknowledge that Steamer wasn't good "for a girl," she was just plain good. In 1996, she joined the Toy Machine team. The same year, when asked to appear in the video *Welcome to Hell*, she filmed all of her tricks in just one week. For most of her career, she progressed at the same feverish pace: she caused a sensation in a second video filmed in 1998 and was among the characters featured in the video game *Tony Hawk's Pro Skater* in 1999. She then joined Baker, where she featured in two videos, in 2000 and 2003. As if that weren't enough, she took home four consecutive gold medals at the X Games, from 2004 to 2008. Now she splits her time between skateboarding, surfing, playing music, and her Gnarhunters project, which combines photography and clothing design.

Her moment of glory In 1998, Elissa Steamer became the very first professional female street skater.

The Dynamo

Jason Dill

Nationality	Born	Nickname
American	**1976**	**"Dill"**

His story If Jason Dill has a hard time sitting still, his chaotic childhood might have something to do with it. By the age of seventeen, he had already moved twenty-two times. But one thing in his life remained constant: his love of skateboarding, for which he showed a particular talent. The riders he shared his first sessions with included Ed Temple, future professional skater and founder of the brand Toy Machine, who would go on to become a critically acclaimed photographer. Birds of a feather flock together, and Jason Dill also had an artist's disposition. For many years, he was sponsored by Alien Workshop, a brand that cultivates an experimental, psychedelic image. Intent on doing things his own way, Dill left his native California, considered the El Dorado of skateboarding, for New York. There, he tried his hand at painting, photography, and fashion, eventually creating two brands in 2014: Fucking Awesome and Hockey. He has since returned to live in California and still runs his successful companies, while also pursuing his creative projects.

His moment of glory It's a short step from the skatepark to the college campus: in 2020, Jason Dill was invited by Arizona State University to speak before a crowd of captivated students.

The Jack of All Tricks

Stevie Williams

Nationality	Born	Nickname
American	**1979**	**"Sabu"**

His story　　　　　　　Stevie Williams grew up in Philadelphia, where he cut his teeth as a skateboarder. He had undeniable talent but was met with hostility from passersby. He and his friends were called "dirty ghetto kids" in the neighborhood where they skated. But he didn't let such prejudice stop him; he persevered and went on to join the Element brand. When he was just fourteen years old, he hitchhiked to California to start his career and showed up at Element's Costa Mesa headquarters, much to the staff's surprise. Williams then moved to San Francisco, where he found himself homeless; he spent his days skating and looked for a shelter at night. Running out of money, he threw his remaining energy into attracting the attention of Chocolate and DC Shoes, which catapulted him to fame. At that point, he became known for his extraordinary pop (the ability to jump high with the board) and his unique style, which was both elegant and powerful. In 2002, despite his by-then comfortable situation, he risked everything by leaving Chocolate to start his own brand, Dirty Ghetto Kids. His bet paid off, and DGK was so successful that he was able to establish his own distribution company, The Kayo Corp.

His moment of glory　　　　　In 2003, the DC Shoes brand released *The DC Video*, in which Stevie Williams makes a noteworthy appearance. His tricks were edited to a track by Beanie Sigel, a rapper from Williams's hometown of Philadelphia.

The Self-Made Man

Dennis Busenitz

Nationality	Born	Nickname
American	**1981**	**"Schnitzel"**

His story   Born in the US, Dennis Busenitz was just six months old when he moved with his family to Germany. He grew up in Munich, where he started riding. When he was fifteen, Busenitz moved back to the US, to Kansas. Sponsors took notice of him, and he joined the team of REAL Skateboards, a brand distributed by the California-based Deluxe company. For practical reasons, Busenitz settled in San Francisco, and the hilly city profoundly influenced his skating, with its many long, steep streets peppered with low walls and gates. Once he got started on those never-ending slopes, Busenitz developed a powerful, ultra-fast style, performing tricks at speeds that would make other skaters tremble. Whereas some riders push off once to accelerate, Busenitz pushed three, five, or even ten times. This fearless reputation earned him enduring popularity among fans of skateboarding: "In our hearts he is Skater of the Year every year," wrote *Skate Jawn* magazine in 2002. And yet Busenitz is very discreet, shying away from the spotlight as much as possible. For some time now, he's lived an hour's drive from San Francisco and has put his welding skills to use to construct his own skatepark—next to his chicken coop!

His moment of glory   In 2006, Dennis Busenitz developed his pro model skate shoe with Adidas. Inspired by the Copa Mundial soccer shoe, the Busenitz Adidas remains the brand's bestselling skate shoe, year after year.

The Speed Freak

Shane O'Neill

Nationality	Born	Nickname
Australian	**1990**	**"Nugget"**

His story

Shane O'Neill was an athletic kid, eager to practice any sport—cricket, Australian football, cycling—with no particular preference. But the day he tried out skateboarding for the first time, his world changed. Besides the freedom he felt on the board, he appreciated the difficulty of the sport. Which is paradoxical, to say the least, since O'Neill has earned a reputation as a gifted skater over the years. The precision of his tricks coupled with his deadpan expression create a disconcerting impression of ease. *Jenkem* magazine even went so far as to suggest that Shane was a robot. His almost superhuman composure has won him first place in many contests, including the Street League—he was added to its prestigious 9 Club, whose members have been awarded a score higher than 9/10 for their tricks. Today, O'Neill runs his own brand, April, which he founded in 2018, and continues to wow skateboarding connoisseurs by regularly publishing videos in which he pushes the limit of nonchalance on four wheels.

His moment of glory

Shane O'Neill is one of the rare riders to have achieved skateboarding's equivalent of a Grand Slam, by winning the X Games, the Street League, the Tampa Pro, and the World Skateboarding Championship.

The Perfectionist

Letícia Bufoni and Rayssa Leal

Nationality	Born	Nicknames
Brazilian	**1993 and 2008**	**"Fats" and "Fadinha do Skate" (the little fairy of skateboarding)**

Their story   Despite their fifteen-year age gap, Letícia Bufoni and Rayssa Leal experienced the same rise to fame as child stars. Both learned to skate in their native Brazil before traveling around the world to compete, winning medal after medal. Bufoni paved the way, taking home six gold medals at the X Games. One day, she heard about a video that had gone viral: it featured a seven-year-old girl dressed as a fairy, skating in a tutu. More than her outfit, it was the budding rider's astonishing skill that had everyone raving. Even Tony Hawk weighed in. The young prodigy was Leal, and it turned out that her idol was none other than Bufoni. A meeting was eventually arranged between the two skaters, and Bufoni became Leal's mentor. In the years that followed, they went from contest to contest together, celebrating their respective victories. The crowning moment came in 2021, when Leal took home the silver medal at the Tokyo Olympic Games, and Bufoni was there, front and center, to congratulate her. She's one teacher who doesn't mind a bit being outshone by her student.

Their moment of glory   Like Rayssa Leal and her tutu performance, Letícia Bufoni had her own viral video featuring her "Sky Grind." In 2022, she was filmed skating in a military aircraft at an elevation of more than 9,000 feet (2,750 meters), before parachuting out of the plane on her final trick.

Facing page   Letícia Bufoni (top) and Rayssa Leal (bottom).

The Queens of Brazil

Nyjah Huston

Nationality
American

Born
1994

Nickname
"The Soul Crusher"

His story
Born in California, Nyjah Huston had an unusual childhood. Under the guidance of his father, he was homeschooled and raised in the Rastafarian tradition. At his father's insistence, he took up skateboarding at the age of five and progressed by leaps and bounds. When he was eleven years old, Huston participated in his first X Games, and he won a gold medal at the age of fourteen. But this impressive debut was cut short: Adeyemi Huston, the family patriarch, relocated to Puerto Rico, taking Nyjah with him. The boy's sponsors were unhappy with the move, because their protégé was no longer available to fulfil his promotional obligations. However, after his parents divorced, Nyjah went to live with his mother in California, where he resumed his career and became a veritable contest-winning machine. He trained like a top athlete and adopted the same style. Wearing compression shorts and basketball jerseys, Huston looked more like an NBA star than a cool rider, which aroused mockery from some skateboarding traditionalists. Preferring to ignore the gibes, Huston let his talent speak for itself, and he became a major figure in modern skateboarding. In 2021, he participated in the first ever Olympic skateboarding competition, but didn't make it to the podium. In 2024, he changed tactics and won the bronze medal in Paris. Fresh from his victory, he returned to the streets to film new breathtaking tricks, confirming his dominance across disciplines.

His moment of glory
To this day, Nyjah Huston remains the most decorated skateboarder in history, all contests combined.

The Skater Athlete

Yuto Horigome

Nationality
Japanese

Born
1999

Nickname
"Yuto"

His story   Yuto Horigome grew up in Tokyo with his two younger brothers. Their father, a taxi driver, was a former skateboarder who had them riding before they could even walk. Horigome was steeped in skateboarding culture from childhood, but that didn't mean things were easy for him; considered noisy and destructive in Japan, the skateboard he loved so much was frowned upon in the streets of Tokyo. So, he had to make do with skateparks, where he trained relentlessly. Eager to try his tricks elsewhere, Horigome started traveling to the US when he was fourteen, and settled permanently in California when he was sixteen. Bolstered by his years of hard work, he won many contests and started skating professionally for Nike and April Skateboards. In 2021, he participated in the Tokyo Olympic Games and won the gold medal on his home turf. His win took him to a new level of fame, and he is now considered one of the best skaters in the world. Unfazed by the pressure, he won gold again in 2024, in Paris, leaving his competitors in the dust.

His moment of glory   In addition to being the very first Olympic street skateboarding champion, Yuto Horigome is also the first skater to win Olympic gold twice.

The Olympic God

Aurélien Giraud and Vincent Milou

Nationality	Born	Nickname
French	**1998 and 1996**	**"Air Giraud" and "Milou"**

Their story   Aurélien Giraud had all the makings of a child prodigy. He started skateboarding when he was five years old and won his first competition two years later. Driven by an insatiable hunger to improve, he trained in his native city of Lyon, on a spot by city hall known by local riders as HDV, for "hôtel de ville." Without waiting for his sponsors to release their official promotional videos, he posted his performances on his own social media profiles, leaving the world dumbstruck by his acrobatic feats. Vincent Milou, another highly talented Frenchman, was born in the Landes region and also started skating young. He was only fifteen when he won the French skateboarding championship—an achievement he would repeat five times. In addition to skating skills, Milou has a way with ideas: he landed a pro athlete sports liaison job with SNCF, the French national rail company, which lets him travel free of charge around the country to check out spots in various cities—a clever way to combine business with pleasure. In 2021, he failed to make it onto the podium at the Tokyo Olympic Games, finishing in fourth place, but made up for it at the X Games in 2022, where he took home a silver medal.

Their moment of glory   Like all self-respecting Frenchmen, Aurélien Giraud and Vincent Milou are also fashion icons. Giraud is the face of Dior, and Milou was part of a campaign for Lacoste fragrances.

Above   Vincent Milou.

Facing page   Aurélien Giraud (left) and Vincent Milou (right).

The French Connection

108

Skate

A skater is always a skater, whether on or off the board. With skateboarding lore to discover, spots to visit, and unwritten codes to learn and respect, skateboarding encompasses all aspects of life. From shopping to eating, and from travel to etiquette, skateboarding is more than an activity—it's a mindset and a lifestyle.

Life

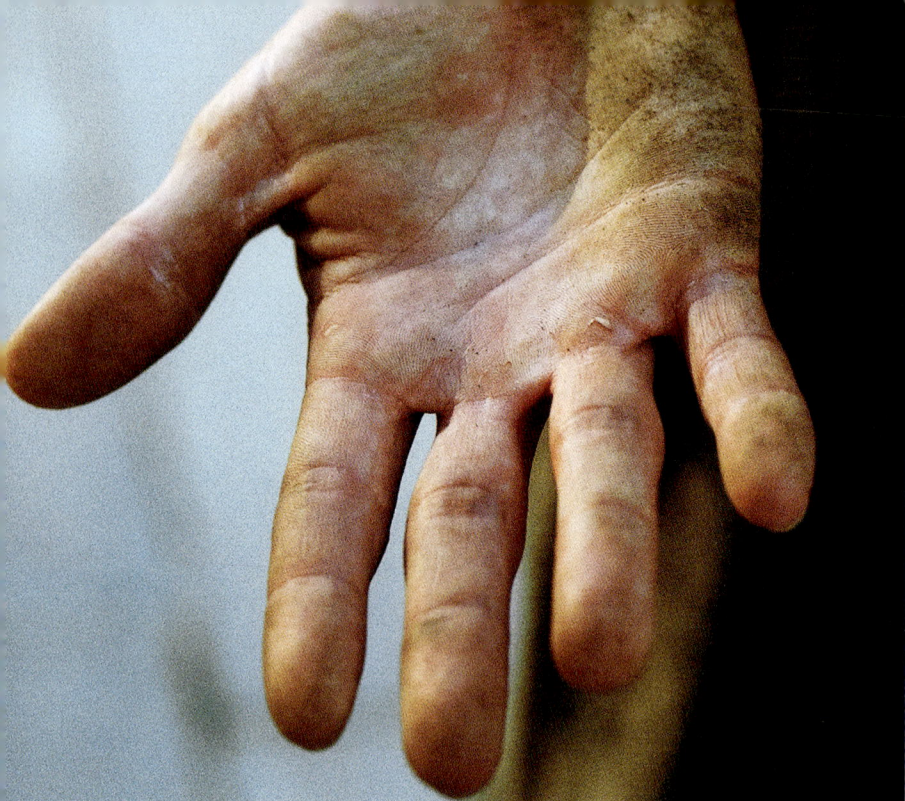

A Sport

Pushing, jumping, spinning, running, falling, getting back up—skateboarding is definitely an athletic activity that puts the body to the test and requires participants to be in good shape. But is it a sport? Several decades after skateboarding's inception, the question remains difficult to answer. Especially since there are almost as many different responses as there are riders.

Rejecting the rules

One of the most common reasons that skaters cite for taking up the activity is a certain ennui with "traditional" sports, such as soccer, basketball, and tennis, and the constraints that come with them: sticking to a fixed training schedule, following a coach's orders, participating in competitions, and pursuing rankings, to name but a few.

For those looking for less pressure and more freedom, skateboarding offers an escape. It has deep roots in community, with friends skating together, encouraging one another, and celebrating each other's successes. There's no offense or defense, just a desire to improve: the only battle to be won is with yourself, when trying to master a new trick. While some of the most talented riders eventually join the competition circuit, this is by no means a requirement for building a reputation. Many renowned riders are happy filming their solo performances in the street, never comparing themselves to others.

Not-so-healthy living

Skateboarders don't always treat their bodies like temples. Some riders manage to perform despite a host of unhealthy habits, but the flip side of this attitude is increased risk of injury and rapidly declining physical fitness. Historically, riders haven't given much thought to what they eat, either: at skate spots, riders refuel on sandwiches, pizza, and burgers. Likewise, many of them skip warming up before skating and stretching after a session. And you won't see them wearing technical clothing designed to improve performance; simple jeans and a cotton T-shirt will do.

Skateboarding and competitions: a love-hate relationship

In the early days, skateboarding relied on structured competitions to develop. To grow beyond its novelty status, it needed to become more organized and attract greater interest from the general public— both of which were made possible by the many championships that were established between the 1960s and 1980s. These events were also opportunities for riders to meet each other, and form friendships and partnerships that gradually shaped the foundations of the skateboarding industry.

But as street skating and specialized media emerged, competitions exerted less influence, to the point that many skaters began to avoid them altogether. A rift appeared

or Not?

between hypercompetitive riders and those who preferred to earn their stripes in the street. There is still the financial argument for participating in contests: the prize money that comes with titles and medals can reach into the tens of thousands, or even hundreds of thousands of dollars. Enough to persuade even the most reluctant riders.

The major contests

Skateboarding contests are made up of two events: the run and the best trick. The run is the equivalent of figure skating's free skate segment; skateboarders have forty-five seconds to perform a series of tricks of their choosing as fluidly as possible. The best trick phase focuses on a single trick, and rewards difficulty and maximum risk taking. In a contest, each rider has three attempts at the run and five for best trick, scored by a panel of judges. The highest scores from each event are added together to reach an overall score and establish a ranking. While slamming is not grounds for elimination, it is heavily penalized.

Over time, various contests have become the benchmarks against which riders measure their talent. In the 1990s and 2000s, the X Games dominated the field by bringing together several action sports in one event (BMX, rollerblading, motocross, and more, in addition to skateboarding). It has since been eclipsed by other competitions, and now the X Games is trying to reinvent itself by offering new challenges that are more in line with the tastes of younger generations, such as video parts filmed in real urban environments and submitted online to viewers who can vote for their favorites.

Today, the most important skateboarding competition is without doubt Street League Skateboarding, created in 2010 by former professional skater Rob Dyrdek. Street League is similar to Formula 1 Grand Prix competitions: it hosts regular face-offs between riders all over the world, giving competitors the chance to accumulate points on the circuit. Once a year, a kind of "grand prix" called Super Crown is held to determine the champions. This new system along with courses that more closely resemble an urban environment have led to Street League attracting the best skaters in the world, including those who usually turn their noses up at contests.

Other less serious but equally popular formats include the CPH Open: an annual event held in Copenhagen that sees skateboarding's biggest stars skate obstacles set up around the city, surrounded by ecstatic crowds. Even wilder still, the Glory Challenge, organized by Dime, features zany obstacles, and the Halloween Hill Bomb, created by *Thrasher* magazine, involves costumed competitors skating down hair-raising slopes.

Paradigm shift

In the last few years, some skateboarders finally seem to have accepted the idea of being considered athletes and have adopted a corresponding lifestyle. The youngest riders watch what they eat and have traded the six-packs guzzled by older generations for water or ginger shots. And to extend their time on the board, older skaters now rely on a set of best practices that includes stretching, massages, cold showers, and soothing balms—anything that will help them stay skating. This is reflected in the average age of riders found at skate spots; it's no longer rare to see people in their fifties or even sixties catching air.

Skateboarding's inclusion in the Olympic Games has also made a huge difference: twenty years ago, many would have viewed this as a concession, but today it is accepted by all. Olympic skateboarders—now considered to be on a par with the greatest champions—train like true athletes and receive support from seasoned coaches, allowing them to push the limits of their performance even further.

Facing page — American rider Tom Asta during a run at Street League.

Below — Steve Caballero at a contest in Visalia, California, 1987.

Guess What? Rider Neen Williams is a perfect example of the lifestyle changes adopted by many skaters. Early in his career, Neen was notorious for his unhealthy habits, but following an injury he decided to get sober and take charge of his health so he could continue skating to his highest potential. Today, he is a full-fledged health influencer, posting fitness videos and recipes for protein smoothies on social media.

A Question

Above It's not always easy for skateboarders to share the streets with pedestrians, cyclists, and scooters.

Facing page It's good form to ask permission from the other skaters at a spot before putting wax on an obstacle.

Skateboarding is generally perceived as a fun and open-minded activity, but it's still governed by a system of rules. Over time, riders have decreed a long list of dos and don'ts, and have been known to clash at spots with other wheeled users.

# of Et

Code of conduct

The rules governing skateboarding can be divided into two categories: etiquette and taste.

In terms of etiquette, the most obvious rule is that when you get to a spot, it is customary to greet other riders, even those you don't know. However, it is highly frowned upon to "snake" someone, in other words to skate an obstacle without waiting your turn. Some customs are more nuanced, but are still worth following. For example, when someone attempts a trick and fails, it's considered rude to perform the same trick next to them; you may come across as a show-off. Something else to be aware of: you shouldn't put wax on an obstacle without asking other riders first, because it will change the way they have to approach their slides.

Rules regarding taste are more subjective and sometimes border on snobbery. One faux pas that has riders in almost unanimous agreement is the "mall grab," which involves carrying a skateboard by a truck rather than the deck. This gesture is named after teenagers who wander shopping malls flaunting brand new skateboards, which they almost never use, just to look cool. A thornier subject concerns "illegal" tricks, which are supposedly too easy or unaesthetic, and therefore rejected by most riders. Some skaters push back against this judgment, however, which runs counter to skateboarding's inherent free spirit.

Skaters' frenemies

Skateboarders aren't always very accepting of people who practice other roller sports, and never is this more obvious than in their interactions at spots and in skateparks. First, there are the BMXers, considered a danger to the public; colliding with one of these hurtling bikes hurts like hell. Then come the rollerbladers—renowned cheats. How dare they parade about with their wheels attached to their feet, when riders have to keep their boards under control at all times? And finally, we have the scooters, a skateboarder's sworn enemy. Often straddled by reckless "scooter kids," these are considered a nuisance by the vast majority of riders.

Guess What?

The brand Toy Machine released skateboard decks emblazoned with a "no scooter" sign on the bottom, making no bones about its dislike for the vehicle.

iquette

A World of Spots

Over time, riders have invented their own geography. Instead of countries and cities, they talk about addresses, locations, and topography— all informed by a single question: where can we skate? In answer to that question, they've compiled a constantly expanding list of spots suitable for skateboarding.

Local culture

In every city, riders find places where they can practice regularly. These are most often large esplanades dotted with urban fixtures, such as the seafront at Venice Beach, in Los Angeles, or the Place de la République, in Paris; but riders may also appropriate less expansive locations. These places become meeting points for skaters in the area, who ultimately develop a highly detailed knowledge of their topography. These riders are able to point out the slightest irregularity on the ground, know if two seemingly identical benches are actually of different heights, and can tell if a slab of concrete that is poorly attached to a low wall might cause a fall. These budding urbanists are called "locals"—a prestigious title earned through consistent practice. It can take skating in the same place every week for months, or even years, to attain this rank.

A skateboarding paradise

Smooth ground, plenty of obstacles, mild weather: some places seem made to attract skaters from around the world. The global hotspot remains Los Angeles, with 260 days of sunshine a year and a spot on every corner in the form of stairs, benches, inclines, schoolyards, and more. The City of Angels is also where most skateboard brands and distributors are headquartered, so riders can kill two birds with one stone. San Francisco is another California dream. With historic skateboarding spots and countless hills, it's the favorite stomping ground of speed freaks. On the East Coast, New York is also popular with riders, despite less sun and a grittier urban environment. In Europe, Barcelona has modern architecture and a certain tolerance of skateboarders—who are viewed negatively in some other cities—making it a mecca for riders. More recently, skaters have set their sights on the Chinese city of Shenzhen, whose numerous squares full of low granite walls and steps make it a giant city-sized skatepark. It's become so popular that many brands have made Shenzhen a stop on their teams' tour schedules.

The quest for the "NBD"

To reach the highest summits of skateboarding's global pecking order, riders have to prove themselves at iconic spots known for their difficulty. Much like surfers will travel to ride a famous wave, riders will seek out a must-skate handrail, a set of steps, or even a simple bench. The most famous of these destinations are given nicknames: there's El Toro, in Lake Forest, California; Jaws Blocks, in Louisville, Kentucky; Le Dôme, in Paris; and Paral-lel, in Barcelona. The most talented skaters dream of leaving their mark on these spots, but there's only one way to do so: perform an NBD: a "never been done." An NBD is a trick that has never been performed at a given spot, so pulling one off can, if captured on video, catapult a rider to fame.

Facing page   For decades, skateboarders have occupied the Esplanade du Trocadero, in Paris.

Above   The Museum of Modern Art in Barcelona (MACBA) is the Catalan capital's most famous spot.

A heritage under threat

To the chagrin of skateboarders, some spots end up being reconfigured or even destroyed. Many public and private entities, irritated by the noise associated with skateboarding and concerned about potential injuries, take measures to prevent riders from using certain spots. This happened at a car wash on Sunset Boulevard, in Los Angeles, where daring riders would jump from the roof to carve a sloping wall below. The car wash in question has since installed barriers around its property to discourage daredevils. But the resistance is mobilizing: in London, Southbank locals managed to save their favorite spot from destruction by launching an online petition. Even crazier, rider Josh Kalis—a local luminary at Philadelphia's defunct Love Park—salvaged granite slabs from the spot where he spent his youth and used them to build a skatepark.

In its Seoul store, London brand Palace recreated the columns from the Southbank spot in tribute to the British skateboarding landmark.

Below   Paris's Place de la Bastille has recently become one of the most popular skateboarding spots in France—or even the world.

Facing page   Skaters the world over seek out the same obstacles: benches, low walls, and stairs.

The Skate Shop: A Ha

The skate shop is where you head to discover new products, get advice from seasoned riders, and run into local greats. Every rider has fond memories of the first time they set foot in one of these temples of skateboarding culture.

Guess What?

Skateboards come in a range of widths, expressed in inches (7.75", 8", 8.5", etc.). Although the difference between sizes is minimal, each rider has their favorite format, which they value for certain qualities. Narrower boards are known to be easier to handle, but leave less room for error. Wider boards are heavier, but better suited to a wide variety of spots.

∧ven
for
Enthusiasts

More than a store—a gateway

It can be intimidating to take up skateboarding. Besides the fear of not being any good, there's the embarrassment of being an unknowledgeable rookie, which can make choosing equipment difficult. Luckily, skate shops are there to assist aspiring riders. Many of these stores sell complete boards, sometimes even in smaller sizes for children. However, most people buy a custom build: they choose the deck independently from, and along with, griptape, trucks, bearings, and wheels. Besides the transactional aspect, a visit to a skate shop is also an opportunity to leaf through the latest magazines, meet other skaters, discuss with enthusiasts, ask for advice from the sales staff, check out products in real life that you've only seen in videos, rub shoulders with local stars—in short, immerse yourself in the world of skateboarding.

Facing page   Every skate shop carries a wide assortment of brands and decks in different sizes.

Right   Storefront of the Vega skate shop in Paris.

More than a store—an icon

A few skate shops have evolved from mere stores into major institutions. One example is FTC, a store in San Francisco that grew from humble beginnings. Opened in 1986 as part of a ski and tennis shop, FTC expanded until it was able to open its own store in 1994; in the process, it became the essential meeting place for the city's skaters. The skate shop went on to be the primary sponsor for many of the sport's future legends, who still express their gratitude for that initial leg up. Nowadays, decks designed by the most illustrious riders of the last few decades decorate FTC's walls, proof of its ability to stay relevant.

Other cities around the world have their own versions of these stores, loved by generations of riders: London's Slam City Skates, Berlin's Titus, and Melbourne's Fast Times, to name but a few. Some skate shops have even more dramatic histories that see them evolve into successful brands. The most famous of these, of course, is Supreme: in the last thirty years, it has gone from being a small store on Lafayette Street in New York to a streetwear empire valued at more than a billion dollars.

Above   Skate shop sales staff take the time to find out about the customer's practice, level, and personal preferences before proposing different deck or wheel models.

Left   Selection of skate shoes. High-top shoes provide ankle protection, while lower cut models prioritize freedom of movement. Regardless of the style, all skate shoes have to withstand wear and give the rider good control, known as boardfeel.

Facing page   Assembling a complete skateboard, from laying the griptape to fitting the trucks and wheels.

Iconic Skate

Skaters are constantly consuming and producing new images in order to learn, to motivate themselves, to promote their practice, or just to be entertained. While the original skateboarding magazines continue to play an important role, they now face competition from new online formats that stoke this appetite for visual content.

Me

From the kiosk . . .

For a long time, print magazines dominated skateboard culture. Through photos and interviews, they communicated the latest news, presented riders to watch, and reported on the wildest recent tricks. Readers also scoured the ads to learn about hot new products. In 1981, *Thrasher* magazine became the ultimate reference worldwide. The magazine flew off the shelves at skate shops everywhere, even where English wasn't spoken. Coming a close second, *Transworld—Thrasher*'s main competitor—launched in 1983. In Europe, *Free Skate Mag* held its own against the American heavyweights.

Above   In the mid-1960s, the general press began to take an interest in the skateboarding phenomenon.

Left   *Thrasher* magazine has become a brand in its own right, with a logo as recognizable as any skateboard maker's.

Facing page   *Transworld, Big Brother, Thrasher*—just some of the publications that are essential reading for skateboarding enthusiasts.

...to the screen

In 1993, a variation on print formats appeared in the form of *411VM*: the first video magazine in the history of skateboarding. Each quarter, subscribers received a video cassette tape in their mailbox featuring a variety of "articles," including interviews, portraits, contest roundups, and clips of new riders. This innovative format lasted for a little over a decade, with sixty-seven issues released. Since then, skateboarding media have migrated to computer, tablet, and smartphone screens. *Thrasher* magazine

played its cards right and now has a very popular website and YouTube channel. The Jenkem website serves up nervy content that appeals to a wide audience. For Internet users short on time, the YouTube channel Quartersnacks publishes a weekly selection of the top ten best tricks taken from the latest brand promotional videos, which many fans follow religiously. Finally, most skateboarding stars post their own performances and glimpses of daily life on social media, dispensing with the middleman.

Guess What ?

When it first launched, *Thrasher* magazine was more generalist in tone and published articles on anything slightly related to skateboarding. The cover of the May 1988 issue was even devoted to snowboarding!

dia

Skate
c

A skater is, above all, an aesthete.
From the clothes they wear
to the music they listen to,
or from the design on the bottom
of their board to the way they are
photographed or filmed, riders from
every discipline have an appreciation
for the aesthetic. It's no wonder,
then, that they have forged such
strong ties with creatives from
all fields.

ulture

Skateboarding and Fashion:

The relationship between skateboarding and fashion has taken many forms, from rejection or appropriation to seduction and, finally, collaboration. The two worlds have never been indifferent to one another and, over the years, have grown inseparable.

The all-important look

In the 1970s, skateboarders made a point of standing out from the rest of the population through their clothes. Making a fashion statement while remaining practical, they created a look all their own: ripped jeans, unbuttoned shirts, and canvas shoes (most often Vans). You could identify a skater just by their clothes. From this moment on, clothing and accessories took on an increasingly important role in the skateboarding scene. The primary aim was to assert the difference between riders

and the rest of society: in the early 1990s, skaters' baggy pants created a unique look that contrasted sharply with prevalent formal fashion codes. Who cared what everyone else thought—only the opinion of other skaters mattered. Which brings us to fashion's second function in skateboarding culture: it's a symbol of belonging. How many kids, on the first day of school, have picked out a fellow skater in the crowd by their outfit alone? Skateboarding fashion's third purpose is to draw a distinction between different influences; riders who like technical or daredevil styles, rock or hip-hop music, street or ramp skating don't wear the same clothes, or the same brands, in the same way. For example, you can bet that a rider with a pair of Fallen shoes on their feet probably has little in common with a rider wearing DCs. And finally, a skater's look can enhance their style. All those in the know agree—a trick performed by a fashion forward skater will be all the more impressive!

Mainstream acceptance

To the horror of certain purists, many skatewear items have now become must-have pieces worn nowhere near the skateparks. Some found their way into the closets of celebrities, whose fans quickly followed their lead, creating unexpected mainstream fads. The most obvious example is probably the Thrasher T-shirt, which has been worn by stars like Ryan Gosling and Justin Bieber. Several years before that, the Carhartt beanie got some unexpected publicity when singer Rihanna wore one, making it a hot item. The Fucking Awesome brand has dressed famous figures like Joe Jonas and Sam Smith; its founder, Jason Dill, says he's flattered by this recognition. His attitude isn't shared by everyone, though, and some riders don't appreciate seeing their favorite clothes worn by people who don't skate. They even have a word for them: posers. But this hasn't slowed the spread

A Love Story

Facing page   Skaters of the Bones Brigade in 1986 wearing jackets featuring the Powell Peralta logo.

Above   Actress Farrah Fawcett on a skateboard in her iconic outfit from the series *Charlie's Angels*, 1977.

of skateboarding style among mainstream fashionistas or prevented certain skateboard brands from becoming fashion heavyweights. Vans is a good example: the company's Old Skool and Slip-On styles are worn around the world, by skaters and non-skaters alike.

From fashion to luxury

Although skateboarding and luxury now have a working relationship, it took a while for them to accept each other. It all began with a bit of unauthorized appropriation: to make a show of their irreverent attitude, several skateboard companies parodied the logos of major haute couture brands. DC Shoes, for example, tweaked Chanel's iconic intertwining Cs, replacing one of them with a D; Stüssy made a similar move, replacing the Cs with two letter Ss. In a more recent example, the Canadian brand Dime selected the typeface Cochin regular—Dior's signature font—for its logo.

But these ironic tributes aren't always well received. In 2000, Supreme released a series of boards and accessories covered with a monogram heavily inspired by Louis Vuitton's. Just two weeks after they hit the market, the products were pulled from the shelves following a formal notice from the French luxury brand, which didn't appreciate Supreme taking such liberties. At the time, it was hard to imagine the two brands collaborating one day. But that's what happened in 2017: initiated by designer Kim Jones, then artistic director for menswear at Louis Vuitton, a collection combining the French luggage maker's monogram with Supreme's emblematic red was presented at Paris Fashion Week. It was a critical and commercial success, marking with a bang the official start of a romance between luxury, skateboarding, and streetwear.

Other memorable collaborations based on this model followed: Palace and Gucci, Stüssy and Dior, DC Shoes and Agnès B. Even more surprisingly, luxury brands were now seeking inspiration from skateboarding style for certain products, such as baggy jeans by Céline, or Lanvin's Curb sneaker—a direct reference to the D3 model by skate shoe brand Osiris. Several riders have recently become the faces of major luxury labels: Briana King appeared in *Vogue* wearing Dior, and Carlisle Aikens has strutted down many a catwalk as well as appearing as a model in a Calvin Klein campaign. In 2025, Louis Vuitton made a big show of presenting its new ambassador, New York skater Tyshawn Jones, who is also a member of . . . the Supreme team! What goes around comes around.

 **Guess what ?** Dior held its fall-winter 2022 show on the campus of a university in Seoul, South Korea, where it built a huge set resembling a skatepark. To open the show, a team of ten women skateboarders were invited to show off their tricks before the models took to the runway.

Facing page, clockwise from top left
Tyshawn Jones, Briana King, Evan Mock, Yuto Horigome: it's an easy jump from pro skater to pro model.

Skateboarding on the Silver Screen

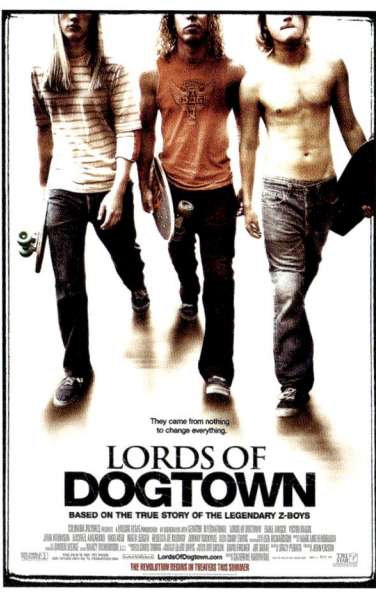

Skateboarding's dynamism and attitude make it particularly videogenic. Whether featured in amateur productions, arthouse films, or even movies produced by riders themselves, skateboards have great screen presence.

Video: an essential tool

Whether it be to document their skating achievements or make themselves known to other riders, every skater has, at one time or another, turned to video. Not so long ago, you needed to have access to a camcorder; sometimes it was borrowed from parents or received as a birthday gift. Now, just about everyone can whip out their smartphone and immortalize any trick. But that doesn't mean there aren't rules about filming. The most important one is to avoid wasting the filmer's time. If you're not sure you can complete a trick after a reasonable number of attempts, don't ask to be filmed.

Video also plays a key role in creating montages called "sponsor-me tapes," which riders send to brands in the hopes that their talent will attract attention. Although videos used to be recorded on videocassettes, DVDs, or USB keys, these physical formats have gradually disappeared and been superseded by content posted on social media.

When riders aren't making their own videos, it's brands doing the work. To promote themselves, brands must regularly publish videos showcasing their team's performance. Each member of their stable is given a "part": a segment lasting several minutes and edited to music. Parts are a bit like the songs that make up an album. The first one is reserved for a new recruit or a promising youth, and the last one for the most skilled skater, who ends the video on a high note. Initially filmed using whatever means were available, these productions have become more professional over time, giving rise to specialized occupations, including camera operators, who must be able to follow their subjects in real time on a skateboard; editors; and directors. These videos are more than a communication tool—they're a driving force of the skateboard industry.

Facing page Filming *Lords of Dogtown*, written by Stacy Peralta and directed by Catherine Hardwicke, in 2005.

Above Promotional posters for *Gleaming the Cube* (1989), *Thrashin'* (1986), and *Lords of Dogtown* (2005).

Skating on the big screen

Skateboarding has inspired many movies, most of which can be divided into three main categories: comedies, initiation stories, and dramas.

Among the comedies, *Grind* (2003) recounts with schoolyard humor a group of skateboarders' dreams of greatness. Bam Margera, the rider made famous on the show *Jackass,* even makes several cameo appearances.

As for dramas, *Gleaming the Cube* (1989) was a trailblazer in the genre. In it, Christian Slater plays Brian Kelly, a young skater investigating his mother's mysterious death. Several years later, *Paranoid Park* (2007) was released. This screen adaptation of Blake Nelson's novel, about a teenager who accidentally kills a security guard in a skatepark, was directed by Gus Van Sant and lauded by critics.

Finally, initiation stories make up the majority of movies about skateboarding. The best-known is *Lords of Dogtown* (2005), which tells the epic story of the Z-Boys, but the genre includes more minor films like *Street Dreams* (2009), starring the rider Paul Rodriguez, and more accomplished works like *Mid90s* (2018), featuring Na-Kel Smith, a member of the Fucking Awesome team.

These onscreen appearances by skateboarding stars are fairly common and have included Tony Alva, Tony Hawk, Christian Hosoi, Steve Caballero, and Rodney Mullen. Numerous riders have imparted legitimacy to films about skateboarding. Some, like Jason Lee and Evan Mock, have become full-fledged actors, while others have stepped behind the camera, such as directors Stacy Peralta and Spike Jonze.

Below   Marty McFly, played by Michael J. Fox, on his famous hoverboard in *Back to the Future Part II* (1989).

Facing page   Stills from the dark *Paranoid Park* (2007) and the road-trip movie *Grind* (2003).

Guess What ? In the video *Yeah Right!*, released in 2003 by Girl, actor Owen Wilson performs an impromptu trick: during a conversation in a parking lot, he suddenly grabs a skateboard and pulls off a daring bluntslide on a railing. But in reality, the Hollywood star did nothing of the sort: Wilson's excellent stunt double was none other than Eric Koston, then a rider at the height of his fame.

Skateboar
and

Music plays a key role in skateboarding culture: it's played at sessions, provides the soundtrack to videos, and can even give a rider the courage to attempt a risky trick. Based on a subtle balance between creativity and mastery, the two disciplines are in total harmony with each other.

An instrument of education

When two riders meet, their first conversation will probably revolve around skateboarding (suggestions for spots, opinions about equipment or the latest popular video, etc.). But the topic is likely to shift pretty quickly to another subject: music. No doubt because most riders discovered their favorite band through skateboarding, which has undeniably shaped the musical tastes of many skaters through the ages. A song used on the backing track for a memorable part in a video, a recommendation from a stranger at a spot, or an album heard in a skate shop are all means by which to discover artists with a more underground sound—a far cry from the standard fare broadcast on the radio and produced by major record companies.

A movement in its own right

Some skaters aren't just satisfied with listening to music as enlightened fans—many of them have crossed over to make music themselves. One of the first to make this happy marriage work was Jef Hartsel, a rider who loves reggae. In 1989, he recorded a song to accompany his own part in the video *Rubbish Heap*, released by World Industries.

Left Los Angeles punk singer Darby Crash, of The Germs, with a board featuring his band's logo.

Facing page The band Sonic Youth has always had close ties with skateboarding culture.

144

ding Music

However, skateboarding soon moved away from reggae in favor of punk, which shared a similar passion for speed and counterculture. The members of Black Flag, for example, were seasoned skateboarders, and the band Suicidal Tendencies, with its song "Possessed to Skate," lent a certain credibility to the skate punk genre. Later, more mainstream groups like Sum 41 and The Offspring also used imagery that drew heavily on skateboarding codes. And who could forget Avril Lavigne's hit single "Sk8er Boi"? In the 1990s, the sport made a detour into grunge with the help of Sonic Youth, which included the rider Jason Lee in the music video for its 1992 song "100%."

And what about rap? Despite having a more marginal presence, the genre is still popular with a large number of skaters. Kareem Campbell—rider and founder of the brand City Stars—even released a rap song, "Time for Some Axion," in praise of his crew.

Nowadays, many professional and retired skaters are trying their hand at music, with some recording albums. Ray Barbee and Tommy Guerrero are two skateboarding legends who have become successful guitarists, and Austyn Gillette has simultaneously pursued a career in both music and skateboarding.

Guess What ?

Vans's famous checkerboard pattern has its roots in music. It was inspired by the black-and-white checks worn by ska musicians to promote racial equality.

Skateboarding: It's an Art

A creative sport par excellence, skateboarding is a powerful tool for aesthetic awakening. It's no surprise, then, that skateboarding has made its way from urban spots to art galleries.

Facing page   Ed Templeton—professional skater turned renowned photographer—at his exhibition at the Los Angeles Museum of Contemporary Art, in 2011.

Right   Mark Gonzales at one of his exhibitions in Seoul, in 2023.

An obsession with images

One of the questions skaters get asked the most is why they give so much importance to the design on the bottom of their deck, when it's only going to get ruined after a few sessions. These ephemeral illustrations will be worn away by constant slides until they disappear entirely, yet they remain the focus of every rider's attention, revealing their artistic sensibility. They are just as important a criterion when choosing a deck as the technical characteristics. Brands have caught on and happily commission renowned artists to come up with designs for them: Shepard Fairey for Powell Peralta, The Andy Warhol Foundation for Alien Workshop, and Kevin Lyons for Girl. Of course, Supreme—the artiest of them all—can pride itself on snagging the most prestigious collaborations. Over the years, the New York-based brand has worked with artists such as Richard Prince, Jeff Koons, Damien Hirst, and Takashi Murakami—a lineup that would make the world's major museums turn green with envy.

In the gallery

Initially recognized for their performances on the board, some riders have also built solid reputations as artists. In 1998, Mark Gonzales, one of the first street skaters, was invited by artist Johannes Wohnseifer to create a skateboard choreography that he performed at the Städtisches Museum Abteiberg in Mönchengladbach, Germany. Since then, Gonzales has pursued his own artistic career through drawing and sculpture, and some of his works are exhibited in Supreme stores around the world. Jason Dill, founder of the Fucking Awesome brand, followed a similar path; today, he combines collage, painting, photography, and drawing. But the skater who has made the most spectacular career shift is undoubtedly Ed Templeton, who traded his board for a camera and became a critically acclaimed photographer.

More recently, Max Palmer—member of the Limosine team—earned fame for his elaborate sculptures made from salvaged materials. Another notable example is Nora Vasconcellos, whose artistic practice began with simple customizations on her own boards; now her drawings are exhibited in galleries.

In 2025, the Théâtre du Châtelet, in Paris, put on *Ollie*, a contemporary stage production that combined skateboarding, dance, music, and architecture.

Basile Lapray, cofounder of Village PM

Recognized footwear specialist Basile Lapray has worked for leading fashion and sportswear brands. An avid rider for many years, he put his expertise to use creating Village PM, a skate shoe brand founded on equal parts performance and aesthetic.

Why did you decide to create Village PM?

I've always wanted to do something related to skateboarding. It's an incredibly diverse field, mostly because there are so many brands, each with something different to offer. Being a huge fan of footwear, I noticed that skate shoes had become more traditional. They used to be a symbolic product, worn all day to indicate belonging to the skateboarding community. Today, many skaters change shoes when they finish a session, opting for dress shoes, the latest sneakers, etc. Skate shoes are becoming just another kind of sports shoe. We wanted to create innovative designs that can be worn proudly outside of an athletic practice. For many years, skate shoes were directly inspired by basketball shoes; later, brands like DC and Lakai released highly technical models featuring elements borrowed from running shoes. We wanted to create a new aesthetic, one based on climbing shoes.

In addition to being sold in skate shops, Village PM products are available in fashion boutiques. Why did you make that choice?

It was important for us to make skaters feel proud about the shoes they were wearing, but we also wanted to make products with designs that would be compelling enough to attract interest outside of skateboarding. Also, it would have been too difficult to limit ourselves to skate shops as our distribution model; we had to diversify our points of sale. But we remain rooted in skateboarding: our communication budget prioritizes our team and our videos.

How important is clothing in skateboarding?

Skateboarding is an intrinsically visual sport: when you skate on the street, you put yourself under the scrutiny of everyone out there. On top of that, skateboarding is very open to all cultural fields, whether it be music, art, or fashion. To me, skateboarding intersects with fashion in several ways—first and foremost as a source of inspiration for designers. Skaters have always developed their own codes to stand out, and many trends have emerged from or been spread through skateboarding culture: baggy pants in the 1990s, cargo pants with elasticated ankles in the 2000s, and, more recently, the practice of taking a pair of scissors to the hem of jeans. Skateboarding also has powerful emotional connotations: it embodies youth, freedom, and rebellion. For fashion brands, these are valuable marketing enhancers that let companies reach a wide audience.

In your opinion, which skaters have the most fashion influence?

That's a good question! I think that a skater's talent spills over into their style and vice versa. I like the way Jerry Hsu and Gino Iannucci dress. Other skaters, such as Ali Boulala and Jim Greco, have contributed significantly to the popularity of slim pants. But the most influential rider has to be Dylan Rieder, who in the 2010s shaped the style of a whole generation.

Facing page   Dylan Rieder, professional skater and model, during a photo shoot in New York in 2013. An influential figure for Basile Lapray, Rieder passed away in 2016, aged twenty-eight, due to complications from leukemia.

148

The Fu

of
Skatebo

uture

Still the same, but always different: that could be skateboarding's motto. Although it remains consistent in its values—freedom, creativity, and energy, among others— the sport continues to reinvent itself to reflect the current moment—and the next.

oarding

More Inclu
at L

Traditionally, skateboarding has always rejected norms, yet it has taken the sport some time to be truly accepting of everyone. The situation has gradually improved thanks to a welcome change in mentality.

usive
ast

Facing page   **Skater Arisa Trew**, pictured here at age fourteen, at the 2024 Paris Olympic Games.

Below (from left to right) Cocona Hiraki, Arisa Trew, and Sky Brown, winners of the silver, gold, and bronze medals, respectively, at the 2024 Paris Olympic Games.

While skateboarding may have developed in opposition to so-called traditional sports and their constraints, it still exhibited some of the same kind of prejudice that plagued other activities. Racing around on a noisy board and performing potentially dangerous moves was something many boys wanted to keep for themselves, convinced that girls were too fragile for that kind of pastime. So, they eyed female skateboarders—who were systematically suspected of being less talented and having less nerve than boys—with a certain distrust when they dared to

set foot in skateparks or spots. Fortunately, trailblazers like Elissa Steamer quickly put these clichés to rest. Today, gender equality has greatly improved, and women skaters are more readily accepted, as illustrated by this quote from skateboarding icon Andrew Reynolds, in reference to Nora Vasconcellos: "She's not my favorite female rider, she's one of my favorite riders, period."

Other prejudices have also been addressed publicly in recent years, especially after rider Brian Anderson came out in 2016. After a successful career, Anderson announced that he was gay and spoke out against a skateboarding culture tainted with toxic masculinity, which created an uncomfortable environment for riders who identify as LGBT. Another glass ceiling has recently been broken by Leo Baker, the first professional transgender skater; he's now sponsored by Nike and feted in the brand's ad campaigns.

The Next

Gener

Skateboarding is a source of inspiration for many, thanks to the skill of the most talented riders, who redefine the limits of possibility on a daily basis. With each new generation, skaters are getting younger and younger, and increasingly gifted.

Fourteen, fifteen, and sixteen: those are the ages of the three young women skateboarders on the podium after the skatepark trial at the 2024 Paris Olympic Games. Awarded the gold, silver, and bronze medals, respectively, Arisa Trew, Cocona Hiraki, and Sky Brown embody a new, incredibly talented generation that gets to benefit from all the progress made by the skaters who came before them.

And they're not the only ones. Every brand team includes young talents eager to prove themselves, some of whom will go on to outperform their mentors. The clearest example is undoubtedly Gui Khury: at just twelve years old, he successfully performed a 1080°—a triple spin at the top of a ramp—at the X Games. Khury performed this feat in front of Tony Hawk himself, who had completed a 900°—a half-turn less—at the very same competition twenty-two years earlier. Hawk rushed to give the young Khury a congratulatory embrace, in what felt like one generation passing the torch to the next.

The future of skateboarding looks bright.

ation

Illustration
Credits

Acknowledgments

I'd like to thank Pascal Monfort for his advice and the loan of his archival material; Juliette Chavarot for her role in the inception of this book; Théo Monelli and Basile Lapray for making themselves available; the whole team at the Vega skate shop for their friendliness and their unfailing dedication to skateboarding culture; Gloria Despioch for her support; as well as Thibault Proux and all the skaters at Bastille for the carefree hours of fun spent in their company.

This book is dedicated to my mother, Patricia.

—Charles Ravinski

The publisher extends its thanks to skaters Hugo Corbin and Jules Rudigoz; photographer Émile Moutaud; author Charles Ravinski; and François Wuest from the Vega skate shop, for their enthusiasm and talent.

This book was created by L'Atelier des Éditions Flammarion—150 years of publishing in Paris.

Flammarion
l'atelier

French edition

Editorial director
Henri Julien

Project manager
Emmanuelle Rolland

Editor
Virginie Maubourguet,
assisted by
Lucia Lefèvre

Design and typesetting
ABM Studio

Illustrations
Éric Doxat

Picture research
Anaïck Bourhis

English edition

Editorial director
Kate Mascaro

Editor
Helen Adedotun

Translation from the French
Kate Robinson

Copyediting
Eleanor Corbett

Proofreading
Nicole Foster

Production
Julie Hautecourt

Color separation
Atelier Frédéric Claudel, Paris

Simultaneously published in French as *Skate Obsession*
© Éditions Flammarion, Paris, 2025

English-language edition
© Éditions Flammarion, Paris, 2025

82 Rue Saint-Lazare
75009 Paris

editions.flammarion.com
@flammarioninternational
latelier@flammarion.fr

25 26 27   3 2 1
ISBN: 978-2-08-048592-2
Legal deposit: 10/2025

Flammarion is actively
committed to reducing
the ecological footprint
of its publications. The
book you hold in your
hands was printed on
paper made from wood
sourced from sustainably
managed forests, using
vegetable-based inks,
by a printer committed to
environmental protection.

Printed in Bosnia
and Herzegovina by GPS